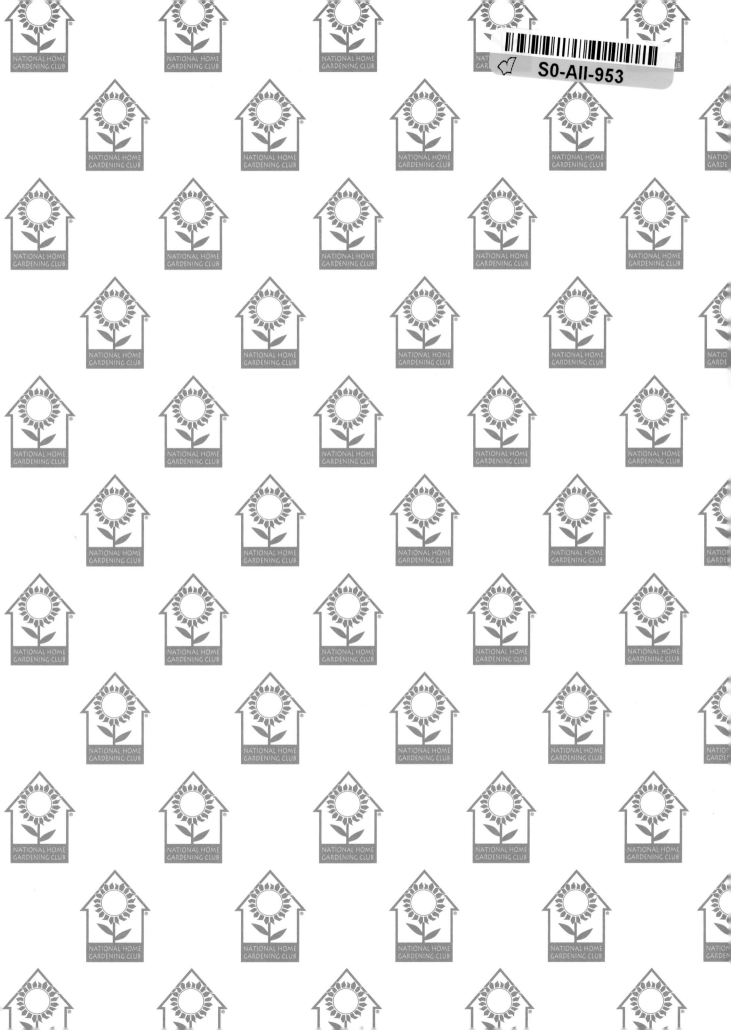

THE PERFECT YARD

NATIONAL HOME
GARDENING CLUB

COMPLETE GARDENER'S LIBRARY™

THE PERFECT YARD

By David Griffin

Printed in 2004.

CREDITS

Tom Carpenter
Creative Director

Mark Johanson
Book Products Development Manager

Dan Cary
Book Production Editor

Michele Teigen
Senior Book Development Coordinator

Dave Griffin
Author

Bill Nelson
Series Design, Art Direction and Production

Mark Macemon
Lead Photographer

Dan Cary, Ralph Karlen
Photography

Craig Claeys
Illustrator

Brad Classen, Carolyn Henry-Johanson
Production Assistance

Carolyn Henry-Johanson
Copywriting & Editing

Contributing Photographers
William Adams, Walter Chandoha, Turfgrass Producers International

Contributing Manufacturers
Lawnboy, Locke Power Reel Mowers, Sylvania Lighting Products, The Toro Company, Union Tools

Special Thanks to:
A-G Sod Farms, Inc., Anderson Irrigation Inc., Brooks Turf, Troy Carson, Gardner Turfgrass, Patten Seed Co., West Coast Turf Farms, Dr. Donald White

NATIONAL HOME
GARDENING CLUB

4 5 6 / 07 06 05 04
ISBN 1-58159-162-4
© 2002 National Home Gardening Club

National Home Gardening Club
12301 Whitewater Drive
Minnetonka, Minnesota 55343
www.gardeningclub.com

The Perfect Yard

Table of Contents

Introduction

A sprawling backyard covered in bluegrass is no more a garden than an Olympic sized-swimming pool is a meditation pond, if one chooses to take the view of the gardening purist. And lawn care is, by anyone's assessment, a markedly different pursuit than cultivating roses or growing herbs. But the lawn, as a feature of your outdoor home, has its place. And, like it or not, the condition and appearance of your yard has an impact on everyone who views the garden areas it frames.

Yard care is not difficult. And with the right information, tools and techniques, it's not even very hard work—or at least, it doesn't have to be. But beyond that, tending your yard can be more interesting and challenging than you may have ever thought. As you become more familiar with the ins and outs of grass selection, for example, you'll find that just as there are virtually endless varieties of annuals and perennials and "garden plants," grass is a wide-ranging and often interesting plant category, too. New varieties are being developed constantly, each improved in some fashion to eliminate a troublesome problem or enhance a desirable quality—and, ultimately, to make lawns increasingly low-maintenance, without sacrificing appearance or hardiness.

In *The Perfect Yard,* you'll find a wealth of information about grass. How to identify it, how to choose it, how to plant it, how to cut it, how to fertilize it, how to heal it, even how to kill it. You'll be introduced to whole new families of tools designed specifically for yard care, but with applications well outside the lawn-mowing realm. You'll also get some good, straightforward instruction on how to care for your yard and garden tools: everything from sharpening a spade to changing the air filter on your gas-powered lawnmower.

In this new book created for our members by the *National Home Gardening Club,* you'll also find extensive discussion of the lawn's closest siblings: border plantings and accent plantings.

Approached from the perspective of the yard as a whole, you may see these simple planting beds and sometimes-overlooked accents from an entirely new perspective. They are important features that define and unite all at once. A host of tips and advice on yard maintenance is included as well: everything from pruning trees to winterizing woody shrubs.

However you view your yard, it is a community of plants that fulfill a purpose or purposes. You can stroll through it and feel the morning dew on your feet. You can watch your children or grandchildren frolic across it. You can host party guests on it. You can throw down a lawn chair and read a good book on it. There is plenty that a nicely designed, well-tended yard can do to improve your quality of life.

Here is the biggest secret behind developing your skills and building your motivation when it comes to yard care: Make your yard into one that's worth caring for. With this in mind, consider *The Perfect Yard* a practical guide to creating the yard that works for you. However simple or ornate, a landscape you create is one you will care for with the most joy and effectiveness.

IMPORTANT NOTICE

For your safety, caution and good judgment should be used when following instructions described in this book. Take into consideration your level of skill and the safety precautions related to the tools and materials shown. Neither the publisher, North American Membership Group, Inc., nor any of its affiliates can assume responsibility for any damage to property or persons as a result of the misuse of the information provided. Consult your local building department for information on permits, codes, regulations and laws that may apply to your project.

Make coming home an aesthetic experience. A rich variety of colors and textures in the landscape are a beautiful complement to your home, adding to its value and providing a welcome that extends beyond your front door.

Name your desire: an inviting path meandering through flowering shrubs, a broad park-like lawn on a summer evening, or the secret-garden atmosphere of old-fashioned perennial beds and specimen trees.

Whether creating the rustic simplicity of a woodland theme, or cultivating a cottage garden filled with an abundance of flowers and fragrance, keep an eye on the harmonious balance of landscape elements. A lawn may be a site for play and recreation, but it is also a major design feature in the home landscape and merits consideration beyond simple utility. The gently curving contours of these two lawns set up pleasing rhythms to the border plantings, directing the viewer through the garden and enhancing the aesthetics of the whole.

Attention to detail enhances every area of the yard. A utilitarian path is made beautiful with a few well-chosen plantings. A backyard flower bed abandons conventional rectilinearity to stunning effect. Even the traditional broad lawn becomes a private retreat when bordered by hedges and a screen of specimen trees.

DESIGNING A NEW YARD:
An Exercise in Practical Imagination

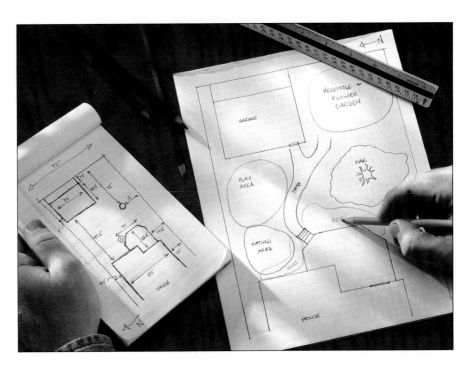

Have you ever tried to imagine a brand new yard? It's sometimes hard to see past the forty-foot oak and the barbeque pit that are already there. But you can still see that there is room for improvement. So, where do you start?

The secret to visualizing new yard features is to do it on paper in a spot where you can't look at the real thing. This is useful even if you aren't intending to do a whole yard makeover, because it allows you to make small advances towards a bigger goal, rather than an assortment of individual projects that don't work together.

First, put the permanent features of your yard on graph paper. Measure off the house and lot lines first, and then corroborate measurements by checking distances between other features. Decide on a scale and transfer all the measurements to the graph paper with pencil, so you can erase. Observe the yard for a day and indicate the approximate hours of sun each area gets. Be aware of how this will change if trees will be coming down and as the angle of the sun changes with the seasons.

Forget about your existing yard and visualize the "stage" you have on paper. Think about your needs and the needs of your family. What effect do you want to create? Where are the best places to meet the various needs of the yard's users? Don't worry about specifics yet, just get the general features down. For example, block in the play area, the utility area, the nature/retreat area, the vegetable garden—you decide how you want to set the space up. After drawing things in on paper, go back to the yard with some flags or marking paint to see if your ideas still make sense at life size.

Using the actual space and your map as a reference, figure out in broad terms how those general areas will be defined. Pencil in the tall hedge, drop in the ground-cover under the tree, draw the curves for the border plantings. Try not to create numerous small islands of lawn that will be difficult to mow, but don't be afraid to reduce the size of a lawn; it will save you time in the long run. Remember that even "shade-tolerant" grasses like to have three or four hours of direct sun a day. Be prepared to sacrifice grass to a low light groundcover, pavers, or mulch in shady areas.

Now, decide what to plant. Your plan may indicate broadly that you need a hedge here, a tree there, and a low bed of flowering plants there, but which species do you select from these broad categories? How many of each will you need? Go to a reputable garden center and get help. Importantly, know the square footage of each planting area you intend to fill, be conscious of the colors of existing plants and structures, and know how much direct sunlight each area gets. You may want to get design advice from an expert at the garden center or a hired landscape architect. Once you've got a plan you like in your mind and on paper, you're halfway home.

Taking accurate measurements and experimenting with shapes, sizes and ideas are important parts of planning you new yard.

Yard Care Tools

The best advice for tool buying is the same for yard care tools as it is for workshop tools: buy the best quality tool you can afford. But make your choices wisely. A well-stocked garden center will happy to sell you a tool for just about any purpose. Use some discretion, and keep in mind that many of the more expensive yard care tools are available for rental.

What to look for in hand tools. If you want minimum-care tools at a competitive price, don't shy from fiberglass handles. They are strong for their weight and will not splinter and crack. When you do buy wood-handled tools, look for the thickest ash or hickory handles with straight, close grain. Avoid painted handles, since paint may hide poor-quality wood. Plastic components are not necessarily a sign of low quality, especially on low- and mid-priced tools where cheap metal and wood components can be a greater bane than plastic. D-handle grips, wheelbarrow trays, even lawn rake heads, make effective use of higher-grade plastics. Soft rubberized grips can be a nice feature on tools. Look for shovel heads with long steel sockets for the handle, full penetration of the handle in the socket, and possibly an extended tab secured to the handle with a fastener. The blades of hoes, shovels and other high-impact tools should be made of low gauge (thick) tempered steel.

A sturdy wheelbarrow is an investment anyone who even dabbles in yard and garden work should make. Common sizes are 4 cubic feet and 6 cubic feet. Bigger is not necessarily better, though. Choose a size that you can manage easily. Wheelbarrow trays are either heavy-gauge steel or high-impact plastic. For most homeowners, plastic is a better choice: it's lighter in weight and won't rust out as steel can.

Ergonomic tool handles. Many long-handled tools, like shovels and rakes, are available with specially-designed ergonomic handles that allow the user to work in a more upright position, reducing back strain and making the tool more comfortable to use.

Where the handle meets the blade

The weakest spot on most yard tools is the point where the handle meets the blade. Here's a quick overview of the most common attachment methods.

Weakest, and unfortunately quite common, is the *tang-and-ferrule* attachment. Here, a rod-shaped tang inserts into a hole in the end of the handle. A cone-shaped ferrule covers the end of the handle to keep it from splitting, and a rivet (ideally) inserts through both ferrule and tang. Look for a high, one-piece ferrule with a rivet or bolt (not just a dimple) fastener.

Better are tools have a *one-piece stamped steel* blade that wraps around the handle in a high socket. A seam running up the back of the socket and steel of a consistent gauge (thickness) throughout reveals stamped production. Look for long sockets bolted or riveted to the handle and possibly a riveted strap extending even higher on the front of the handle.

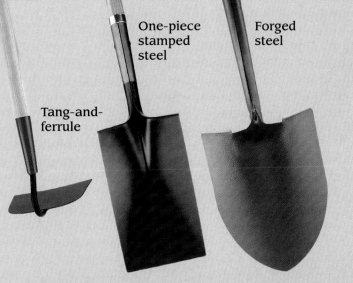

One-piece stamped steel

Forged steel

Tang-and-ferrule

The best tools have a *forged-steel,* one-piece blade and socket. The socket for the handle will have no open seam in the back and the thickness of the steel will vary. Forged tools are expensive, but are worth the price if you'll be using the tool a lot or the tool will come under a lot of stress.

TIPS FOR CLEANING UP YARD WASTE

A light plastic tarp has a multitude of uses around the yard. Lay one out flat as a receptacle for clippings and cuttings, then simply tow them to the compost pile with the tarp. This will not only make cleanup easier, it prevents smaller waste from filtering into the lawn. An 8 × 10 ft., medium-weight, woven poly-ethylene tarp (shown above) is very inexpensive and a good, manageable size.

Don't overload your wheelbarrow. Even clippings and cuttings add up in weight, can become top-heavy, and obstruct vision when piled too high, all of which can add up to a big mess or even injury if the wheelbarrow tips.

Long-Handled Round-Point Shovel: Used for moving, breaking, and turning earth and digging holes for shrubs and trees. Look for a high metal shank, complete penetration of the handle into the shank, and a thick ash or fiberglass handle. The shoulder of the blade should be turned into a footstep. The handle should come to at least shoulder height when the shovel is vertical.

Garden or Edging Spade: D-handled spade with a flat, square blade useful for planting and dividing plants and for cutting edges of lawns. The blade should not flex. The handle should come up to your waist when the blade is resting on the ground.

Long-Handled Square-Point Shovel: Used for shoveling sand, gravel or snow off a flat hard surface. Look for a shoulder-height or greater handle, a high socket and a strong handle.

Drain or Ditch Spades: The narrow blades of a ditch spade and a long-handle ditch spade (curved blade) make them useful for cutting deep, narrow trenches for wire, pipe, or tile.

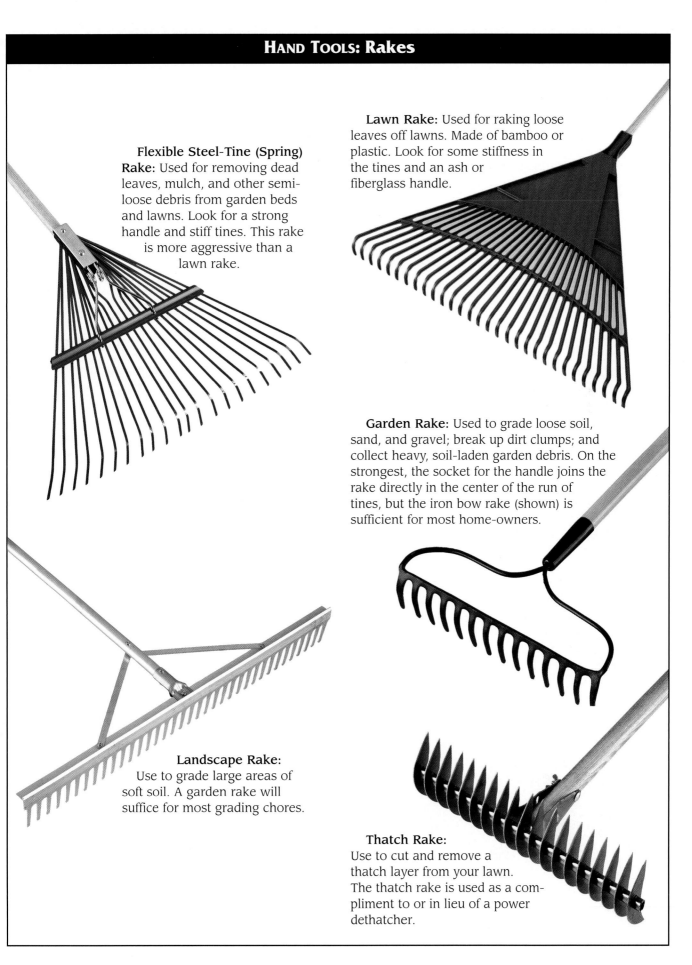

Flexible Steel-Tine (Spring) Rake: Used for removing dead leaves, mulch, and other semi-loose debris from garden beds and lawns. Look for a strong handle and stiff tines. This rake is more aggressive than a lawn rake.

Lawn Rake: Used for raking loose leaves off lawns. Made of bamboo or plastic. Look for some stiffness in the tines and an ash or fiberglass handle.

Garden Rake: Used to grade loose soil, sand, and gravel; break up dirt clumps; and collect heavy, soil-laden garden debris. On the strongest, the socket for the handle joins the rake directly in the center of the run of tines, but the iron bow rake (shown) is sufficient for most home-owners.

Landscape Rake: Use to grade large areas of soft soil. A garden rake will suffice for most grading chores.

Thatch Rake: Use to cut and remove a thatch layer from your lawn. The thatch rake is used as a compliment to or in lieu of a power dethatcher.

Spading or Garden Fork: Used for breaking and turning heavy soils and dividing plants. Look for a high metal shank, with tines that are thick and appear angular or square in cross section. A D-handled fork should come up to your waist when fully inserted in the ground.

Five-Tine Manure or Mulch Fork: Used for pitching manure, compost, mulch, straw, and other fibrous materials. Narrow tines are round, curved, and pointed. Look for durable construction. For pitching fine material, buy a fork with more tines.

HAND TOOLS: Hoes & Cultivating Tools

Hoe: Useful for chopping weeds in the vegetable garden and making troughs for planting seeds. Look for a long handle. Stronger ones have the blade and socket forged out of a single piece of metal.

Scuffle or stirrup hoe: Useful for quickly cutting down young weeds just below the soil level on firm ground in vegetable gardens and on paths. The blade cuts in both directions. Good scuffle hoes have sharp, hard blades that change angle when pushing or pulling to keep an optimum cutting angle. Look for a scuffle hoe that creates a similar angle against the floor when you push or pull it while holding it the way you would in a garden.

Mattock: Useful for removing tough weeds, roots, and young trees when preparing a garden bed. The opposite side can have a pick or an axe-like blade, depending on your needs.

Hand Cultivator: Used to aerate the soil and destroy weed seedlings.

Trowels and Transplanters: Use for planting or transplanting small plants. One or the other can probably serve your needs.

Manual Edger: Trims back grass overgrowth of lawns along sidewalks and other pavements.

Grass Shears:
If you have a great deal of grass beyond the reach of your mower, consider buying an electric string trimmer; otherwise, the time-honored grass shears take care of "nook and corner" grass. Spend a little more to get shears with quality blades that remain tight against one another.

Hedge Shears: For shearing hedges and other plants where many small leaves and twigs are to be cut to one level.

Lopping Shears: For pruning thicker branches and stems. Cuts from 1½ to 2 inch thick woody stems and branches. Get an anvil head when purchasing bargain models since low-end anvil are better than low-end bypass.

Bypass Hand Pruning
Shears: Use for general-purpose pruning of soft and woody plant stems up to ½-in. thick.

Bow Saw: The thin, sharp blade of a bow saw is held under tension by the handle. It cuts thick, green wood easily.

Pole
Tree Trimmers:
This is really two tools—a saw, and loppers—on one long stick for taking out problem branches with both feet on the ground. The loppers work by hooking the branch and levering a lopper blade into it with a rope and pulley mechanism

Draw
Cut Pruning Saw:
Fits in smaller spaces than a bow saw.

Sharpening Garden Tools

Any garden tool that has an edge will benefit from a good sharpening, but none more than tools designed to cut plant material. These include shears of all kinds, along with shovels, spades, hoes and mattocks, which need to be kept sharp to sever roots. It is sometimes necessary to take clippers, pruners, and shears apart to sharpen the beveled and blunt edges: if you do, always secure the blades in a bench vise before sharpening.

A 10-in. flat mill file does a good job of sharpening most garden tools, but a 10-in. half-round file may be needed to file inward bending curved blades, like the blunt, stationary blade of hand pruners. To fine tune sharp-edged tools, glue 300-grit. wet-or-dry sandpaper to a board. Move the back edge of the blade in a circular motion on the paper to remove filing burrs.

TIPS FOR SHARPENING YARD CARE TOOLS

A 10-in. flat mill file will work for sharpening shovels. Avoid oversharpening, leaving the shovel blade dull to the touch (an overly sharp blade will deform quickly with use).

A 10-in. half-round file is used to hone the blunt stationary blades of hand tool such as the loppers shown above. Use long, even file strokes and make sure to maintain the original bevel of all blades.

HAND TOOLS: Tamper

Hand Tamper: Useful for compacting soil in small areas when repairing lawns and for compacting gravel and sand for small masonry projects.

(ABOVE) Protect metal blades by treating them with a protective coat of machine oil. Treat as needed and at least once every growing season.

(LEFT) Use a rotary tool and grinding stone attachment to sharpen larger metal blades. Be careful to maintain factory blade bevels.

Handheld Broadcast Seeder/Spreader: Use to distribute fertilizer, seed and ice-melt for smaller areas where precision is not a high priority.

Push-along Broadcast Seeder/Spreader: Used to rapidly cover larger areas: relatively low precision.

Pump Tank Sprayer: Provides more control than hose-end sprayers for delivery of potentially dangerous pesticides. Do not use the same device for applying fertilizers and pesticides.

Drop Spreader/Seeder: Slower but more precise than broadcast spreaders, drop spreaders permit spreading at very exact rates and with less spill-over into neighboring areas.

Hose-end Sprayer: Container and sprayer that dilutes pesticides or liquid fertilizers to a set ratio of water-to-product. Glass containers are easier to clean thoroughly after use, if you will be changing sprays. More expensive sprayers can be set to apply at different rates of dilution.

Electric String Trimmer: Corded and cordless electric string trimmers are useful for cutting grass near fences, trees, steps and other obstacles. They are clean, quiet, easy to maintain, and relatively inexpensive.

Gas String Trimmer: Useful for trimming very large or multiple properties where a cordless trimmer would lose its charge. Gas string trimmers usually use two-cycle engines, which are louder and more polluting than four-cycle engines. Gas motors require regular maintenance. In most cases, they are slightly more costly than electric trimmers.

TIP: Protect the bark of trees from trimmers with plastic protectors available from garden centers.

HOW TO REPLACE STRING ON A STRING TRIMMER

String trimmers vary in their methods of accepting new string, but most are equipped with a string cartridge spool that is held to the trimmer shaft with a twist-off cap. Remove the cartridge spool and housing (left photo). Pull out old string, then feed the replacement string into the cartridge—often, notches on the spool keep the strings in place until you can insert it back in the spool housing (right photo). Wind the new string into the cartridge. Importantly, wind string in the correct direction, and don't try to install more string on the spools than the manufacturer recommends. Reattach the housing and cartridge (upper inset photo). Read your trimmer manual for specific instructions and replacement string guidelines.

Hedge Trimmers

Electric Hedge Trimmers: Trimmers, available in both corded and cordless models, are useful if you have a large manicured hedge to trim.

Blower/vacuums

Gas-powered blower/vacuums: These relatively new entries into the lawn tool category are used primarily for fall leaf cleanup. When fitted with the blower attachment (attached to the motor housing above), they direct compressed air so you can blow the leaves and debris into piles for easy disposal. By reversing the motor and replacing the blower attachment with a larger vacuum attachment, you can vacuum up the debris, which is collected in a zippered leaf bag much like the dust bags on portable power tools.

ELECTRIC & CORDLESS POWER YARD CARE TOOLS

A quiet revolution is underway in the area of yard care tools. The ear-splitting roar of gasoline engines is giving way to the hum of electric motors. Cordless electric string trimmers and lawn mowers can now run for up to an hour on a charge, making it possible to maintain the lawns of a half-acre lot entirely with cordless electric tools. While cordless electric yard care tools are still relatively expensive, they are coming down in price, and studies show their cost of maintenance and operation is just a fraction of what it takes to run and maintain gas-powered tools.

Gasoline engines still have the advantage of greater power, which is needed, for example, to drive self-propelled machines over hilly terrain and to handle overgrown weeds and lawns. If you choose to purchase gas-powered tools, be prepared to commit to a schedule of regular engine maintenance. Experts say that regular maintenance extends the life of gas-powered lawn mowers by as much as 400 to 500%. See pages 22 to 29 for tips and information on maintaining and troubleshooting gas-powered lawn mowers and outdoor equipment.

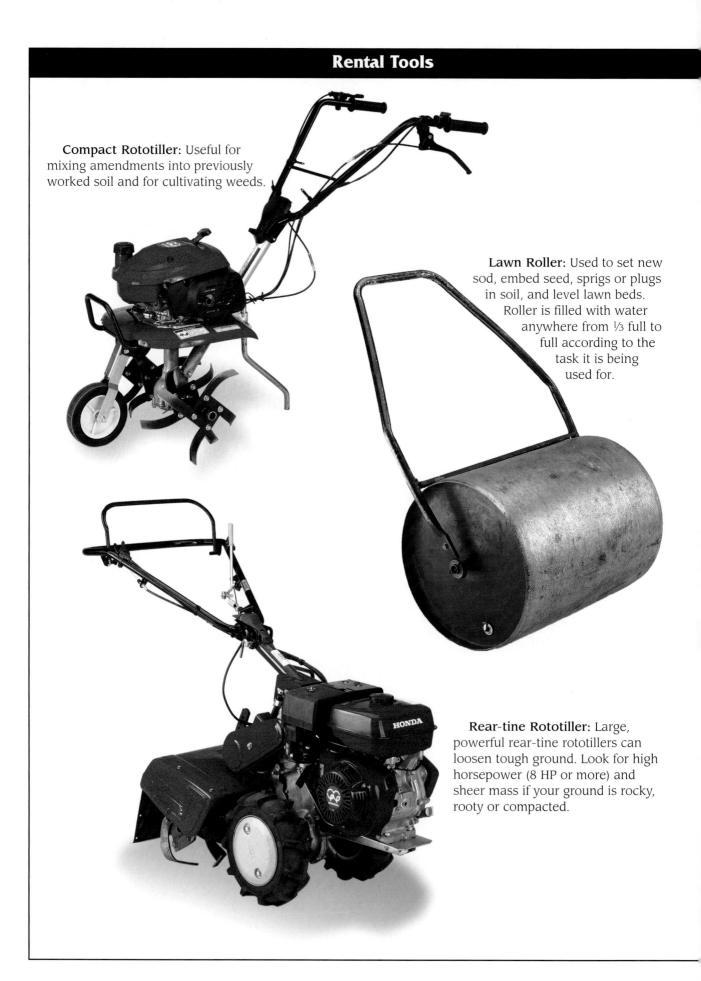

Compact Rototiller: Useful for mixing amendments into previously worked soil and for cultivating weeds.

Lawn Roller: Used to set new sod, embed seed, sprigs or plugs in soil, and level lawn beds. Roller is filled with water anywhere from ⅓ full to full according to the task it is being used for.

Rear-tine Rototiller: Large, powerful rear-tine rototillers can loosen tough ground. Look for high horsepower (8 HP or more) and sheer mass if your ground is rocky, rooty or compacted.

Power Edger: Use for large stretches of overgrown lawn edging against pavement. Use also for cutting narrow trenches for low-voltage electric wires and invisible dog fences.

Sod Kicker: Cuts grass below the soil, leaving slabs of sod that can be rolled up and composted or reused.

Slit Seeder (verticutter): This machine is simply a dethatcher with aggressive, fixed-tine blades and a place to put seed. It's called a slit seeder because it dispenses seeds into the cuts made by the machine.

Power Core Aerator: Aerates soil and encourages breakdown of thatch by pulling plugs of sod and soil to the surface. Avoid aerators with solid tines that just punch holes in the ground.

A Gallery of Lawn Mowers

Riding Mowers: The smaller riding mowers have the engine in the back. Lawn tractors are larger. Garden tractors, the next step up, will operate a wide variety of attachments besides mowers, including loaders, rotary tillers, and log splitters. A garden tractor is shown above.

Rotary Gas Power Mowers: For large or hilly lawns, a gas-powered rotary mower is by far the most popular choice. Gas mowers can power through tough, overgrown warm-season grasses. Self-propelled gas mowers are useful on hilly lawns. On the down side, a gas-powered mower is loud, generates about three times as much pollution per hour as your car, and requires regular engine maintenance. For safety, get a mower with a blade brake on the handle.

Push Reel Mowers: Human-powered reel mowers are enjoying a resurgence in popularity among people with smaller lawns (less than 1,200 square feet). They are quiet, non-polluting, and provide exercise. Plus, they are inexpensive and require very little maintenance. Bargain models are very inexpensive, but you'll find it's worth spending a bit more for a higher-end model.

Cordless Electric Mowers: Cordless electric mowers are growing in popularity due to advances in battery technology. They are quiet, easy to use, and require almost no maintenance. A cordless will cut up to 10,000 square feet of lawn on a charge. Electric mowers are somewhat expensive, but will cost about ⅓ as much to run and maintain as gas mowers. On the down side, electric mowers can have difficulty with tough, dense grasses. Most electric mowers are not self-propelled, which makes them difficult on slopes.

Gas-Powered Reel Mowers: The scissors-like cutting action of reel mowers leaves a finer cut than rotary mowers, and they can cut closer to the ground. However, they are heavier and more expensive than rotary mowers, and usually need to be sharpened and adjusted professionally.

Cordless Electric Robotic Mower: You bury a perimeter wire around your yard and the robotic mower takes care of the rest. These new, "state-of-the-art" mowers work best on relatively flat, obstacle-free yards.

Mulching Blades pull clippings up under the deck and recut them for finer mower clippings.

Regular Blades are used on ordinary, non-mulching, rotary mowers.

A badly damaged blade like the one above cannot be rehabilitated. Replace it.

Safety Tip

LAWN-BOY

Before servicing your lawn mower, always disconnect the spark plug wire from the spark plug.

Lawn Mower Maintenance

A gas lawn mower should last a decade or more, but unfortunately, many don't make it through a third season for lack of proper maintenance. Read and follow the maintenance schedule in the owner's manual, and you will have an efficient, effective and long-lasting machine. Below we list some of the more critical aspects of fueling, oiling and maintaining lawn mowers. Use this information to supplement, not replace, maintenance instructions and machine specifications provided in the owner's manual of your machine.

Riding lawn mowers need the same basic care as four-cycle walk-behinds, but there is a wider variation in how maintenance is performed. Follow the riding lawn mower maintenance routine outlined in the owner's manual.

Sharpening lawn mower blades

Sharpening your own lawn mower blades is a relatively easy job. It doesn't require as much precision as other tool sharpening tasks, and there are a number of sharpening tool options, at least one of which most people will have on hand. You can use metal files, a bench grinder, a rotary tool with a grinding stone attachment, or even a coarse whetstone to put new edges on the blade.

Reel mowers. The blades on most reel mowers need sharpening every year or two, although some of the very high-end models are designed to go 6 or 7 years without sharpening. Have a push mower sharpened professionally or use a kit provided by the manufacturer. *NOTE:* Many reel mower owners assume that, once their mower starts to cut in an unsatisfactory manner, the blades must need to be sharpened. More often, however, they simply need to be adjusted. Reel mowers cut grass blades by capturing them between one of the blades and a flat, horizontal strike bar, then shearing them off. If the gap between the blades and strike bar becomes too big, the mower can't cut effectively. Simply adjust the position of the strike bar so you can hear a very slight tic when each spinning blade passes the bar.

Rotary mowers. Power rotary mower blades should be removed and sharpened at the beginning of every mowing season. Before you do anything else, discon-nect the spark plug wire from the spark plug (See photo, previous page). The best time to work on gas-powered mowers is after they've run out of gas. If there is any gas in the tank, drain it by siphoning it back into your gas can before you start. Then, follow the instructions and photo sequence below to sharpen the blade. Replace or store the blade when finished. If you will be storing the blade for awhile, coat it with machine oil or wax first.

HOW TO SHARPEN A MOWER BLADE

1 Disconnect and ground the spark plug wire and make sure the gas tank is empty. Insert a block of wood into the interior of the mowing deck (or apply a C-clamp as shown here) to keep the blade from spinning during removal. Use a box wrench or ratchet wrench to remove the blade bolt. Remove the blade, keeping all washers and parts in the correct order.

2 Secure the blade in a vise and sharpen with a file, rotary tool or bench grinder. Work to maintain the original cutting bevel on the edges of the blade. When sharpening, the blade should not be sharpened to a knife edge; rather a 1/64-in.-thick edge should be left.

TIP: After sharpening, clean the blade and suspend it from the center on a nail or pegboard hanger to check for balance. If the blade tips so it isn't level, grind down the lower (heavier) side some more on the cutting edge, maintaining the bevel.

3 Reattach the blade to the mower with the bolt and washer. To make sure the blade tracks correctly, measure the distance between one end of the blade and the bottom of the deck, then rotate the blade 180° to see if the other side measures within 1/8 in. of the same distance. If not, you've either got a bent blade (replace it) or a bent crankshaft. If a new blade doesn't fare any better in the 1/8-in.-clearance test, have a lawn mower mechanic service the crankshaft of the machine.

Lawn Mower Engine Maintenance

You don't need to have professional certification in small engine repair to tackle a few basic engine maintenance tasks that are very important to keeping your power mower running well. Anyone who owns a power mower will benefit from having the ability to handle basic engine lubrication, as well as knowing how to replace air filters and spark plugs.

Even routine cleaning of the mower deck and engine will go a long way toward extending the life of your mower. This keeps the cooling fins working effectively and prevents debris from getting into the engine during servicing. If you use water, do not get water in the carburetor. It's better to use an air compressor or a chemical engine cleaner.

See the end-of-season maintenance checklist and lawn mower troubleshooting guides on page 31 for more information.

Cleaning & replacing spark plugs

Remove spark plug with a deep spark plug socket

sized for your plug. Clean the plug carefully with a spray-on plug cleaner, a wire brush and knife, and gap the plug with a round spark plug gauge (See photos, next page). Never use abrasive cleaners on spark plugs. Replace a plug that is damaged in any way or if you are unsure how to service it. Your owner's manual will have the names and model numbers of replacement plugs, the correct gap for your plug electrode, and will also tell you how much torque to use in putting the plug back on. If you don't have a torque wrench, tighten a new plug half a turn past hand-tight and an old plug a quarter turn past hand-tight. Do not put the wire back on yet if you have more work to do.

Cleaning & replacing air filters

Clean or replace the air filter at least once a year. The air filter protects the air intake opening from drawing dust or debris into the engine. When filters become clogged, the flow of oxygen is impeded, disrupting the fuel-to-oxygen burning ratios and resulting in poor engine performance and even damage to the engine. Air filters are either made of foam or paper, depending on the type and model of lawn mower. See page 30.

TIPS FOR LAWN MOWER FUEL MANAGEMENT

Use a fuel stabilizer. Adding a fuel stabilizer to fresh gas can save you big money on repairs to machines by preventing damage caused by old fuel (gasoline that's been in the container for more than two months). Mix a stabilizer into fresh fuel only (stabilizers are ineffective when added to fuels that are already old). Follow the mixing ratios on the stabilizer container.

Get rid of old fuel. To remove old and potentially harmful fuel (more than two months old) from a mower tank, use an old kitchen baster or a siphon. Dispose of the old fuel at a hazardous waste collection site. NOTE: Buying gas on an as-needed basis is the best way to prevent problems associated with old fuel. Use a 1-gallon plastic gasoline can for storing fuel. Be sure to use a non-metallic funnel with a strainer when filling a gas container or tank, and clean around all caps before opening them to keep debris from falling into the tank or fuel container.

How to Replace a Spark Plug

1 Disconnect the spark plug wire from the spark plug and remove the old plug, using a deep-socket wrench sized for your spark plug (sold as "spark plug wrenches"). Avoid touching any part of the plug except the porcelain insulator. Visually inspect the plug to assess its general condition. Light residue on the tip can be cleaned off with a wire brush, but in most cases it's easier to replace the plug—they're cheap.

2 All new spark plugs should be "gapped" before they're installed. The "gap" is the distance from the electrode to the tip of the male-threaded socket of the plug. If you don't have a spark plug gauge to measure the gap, or if you're not confident in doing it yourself, purchase the new plug at a small-engine repair shop. They'll be happy to set the correct gap for you. Hand-twist the new plug into the engine as far as you can, then tighten with the spark plug wrench. Tighten an old plug ¼ turn past hand-tight and a new plug ½ turn past hand-tight. Reconnect the spark plug wire.

How to Lubricate a Gas Engine for Off-Season Storage

2 Replace the spark plug, then very slowly pull the starter rope. You're not trying to start the mower here: only to distribute the oil from the spark plug hole into the engine cylinders.

1 Before you store your gas-powered lawn mower over the winter months, most manufacturers recommend lubricating the engine to protect the cylinder heads. This is a very easy thing to do. Simply remove the spark plug (See photos, top of this page) and squirt about ½ ounce of engine oil into the spark plug opening.

Maintaining two-stroke engines

Some lawn mowers, and most gas chain saws, weed whips and hedge trimmers use two-stroke engines (also called "two-cycle" engines). With two-stroke engines, the fuel/air mix is compressed in and delivered through the crank case. A small amount of oil is added directly to the fuel for lubrication purposes. *You can identify a two-stroke engine by the absence of a separate place to put oil in the engine.* Don't be confused by oil wells for non-engine parts of the machine, such as the bar and chain oil well on chain saws or a gear box oil well on a self-propelled lawn mower. If you have a two-stroke engine, you need to follow special rules for fueling and maintaining the machine. Most importantly, *you must use a mix of gas and two-cycle engine oil to fuel the machine.* Your manual will specify the ratio of oil to gas to use. Add fuel stabilizer to prevent damage caused by old fuel (See page 26).

Two-stroke engine maintenance checklist

(Maintenance procedures will vary from machine to machine.)

- Check for loose bolts and fuel leaks at each use.
- Clean and oil (oil foam filter if specified in your manual) the air filter every ten to 25 hours of operation (See page 30). Replace the filter if you've lost the manual, since cleaning procedures are specific to the engine brand and model.
- Keep the fuel tank full, but completely replace fuel that is old (See page 26).
- Adjust the idle screw according to instructions for your machine if the machine idles fast or will not stay running without applying the throttle.
- Replace or clean and gap spark plug after 50 hours (See page 27).
- Check and clean or replace fuel filter annually.
- Follow applicable winterizing procedures under "End of Season Storage," page 31.
- Clean cylinder head and cooling fins annually.
- Have the machine professionally serviced when the above procedures no longer keep the machine running smoothly.

HOW TO BLEND FUEL FOR TWO-STROKE ENGINES

1 Add two-cycle engine oil to an empty, one-gallon gas container. Use a nonmetallic funnel. In many cases, you can buy pre-measured containers of two-cycle oil for your brand of machine, typically added at a rate of one container per gallon of gas.

2 Add exactly one gallon of regular, unleaded gasoline (preferably, 87 octane or higher and unblended with ethanol or other additives). Secure cap and lightly shake the container to mix the gas and oil.

TIP: If you're having trouble locating the exact type of two-cycle engine oil specified, multi-engine oil mixes are available that claim to work in all two-stroke engines. These may already contain fuel stabilizers.

Maintaining four-stroke engines

Four-stroke engines, like those used in cars, are found on most lawn mowers, snowblowers, large rototillers, and other equipment that sits on the ground or on wheels. Traditionally, this stability is needed because a well or 'sump' of oil needs to stay on the bottom of the engine (as opposed to a two-stroke engine, which can work upside down). Check the level of the oil well every time you add fuel. A fuel-with-oil mix is never used in four-stroke engines. There is always a separate place to put oil.

SAE 10W30 oil works for most four-cycle engines. Use regular, 87 octane unleaded fuel (without ethanol, methanol or MTBE added, if possible). Do not add oil to fuel for four-cycle engines.

Four-stroke engine maintenance checklist

(Maintenance procedures will vary from machine to machine.)

- Check for loose bolts and oil and fuel leaks at each use.
- Clean and oil (oil foam filters only) the air filter every ten to 25 hours of operation. Replace the filter if you've lost the manual, since cleaning procedures are specific to the engine brand and model.
- Keep fuel tank full, but completely replace fuel that is old (See page 26).
- Change oil every 25 hours of operation.
- Adjust the idle screw (if mower has one) according to instructions for your machine if the machine idles fast or will not stay running without applying the throttle.
- Replace or clean and gap spark plug after 50 hours.
- Clean or replace fuel filter annually (if you have one).
- Clean cylinder head and cooling fins annually.
- Follow "End of Season Storage" checklist before winter.
- Have the carburetor adjusted or the machine otherwise serviced when the above procedures no longer keep the machine running smoothly.

HOW TO CHANGE THE OIL IN A FOUR-STROKE ENGINE

1 Change your oil every 25 hours of use. Run engine to suspend particles. Remove the old oil filter (if you have one) with a filter wrench, then drain the old oil into a flat container. Bring the old oil and filter to a service station for recycling.

2 Tighten the oil plug with a wrench. Apply oil to the gasket of a new filter (if required) and tighten one half turn beyond the point where the gasket makes contact. Add the correct amount of oil (see your manual). Run the engine and check for leaks.

TIP: Some motors do not have an oil plug, but must be drained through the fill hole. Before tilting an engine on its side, remove a paper air filter cartridge to prevent oil from the precleaner from soiling the paper.

HOW TO CHANGE A FOAM AIR FILTER

1 Remove the foam air filter. Wash the filter in hot water and a liquid detergent containing a grease cutting agent. Purchase a new filter if the old one is damaged.

2 Squeeze moisture out of the filter by wrapping it in a clean cloth. Then, saturate the filter with engine oil. Squeeze the filter again to spread the oil evenly.

3 After cleaning the parts of the air cleaner assembly, reinstall the filter.

HOW TO CHANGE A PAPER AIR FILTER

1 Remove the paper air filter. You may knock out loose dirt, but a dirty paper filter should usually be replaced. Never wash a paper filter, and do not soak it with oil as you would a foam filter.

2 Some paper filters have a foam pre-cleaner. If instructions allow, these may be washed and oiled. Other foam pre-cleaners may not be oiled. Oiled-foam pre-cleaners will have a mesh barrier that prevents oil from contaminating the paper. Position this barrier against the paper filter when replacing.

Troubleshooting chart for gas-powered lawn mowers

Symptom	Possible problem	Solution(s)
Will not start	No fuel in tank	Add fuel
	Fuel shutoff valve closed	Open valve
	Resistance from blade	Move mower to paved surface
	Starter will not turn (electric ignition models)	Clean and reconnect leads to battery terminals. Check battery, charge if needed
	Fuel line blocked	Replace or clean fuel hose
	Plug won't spark	Clean or replace spark plug or replace shorted spark plug wire
	Engine flooded	Pull with choke open (run position) and throttle closed to dry. Remove spark plug and dry
Low power with smoke and possibly gas smell	Rich fuel mix	Open (turn off) choke all the way, clean or replace air filter (page 30), adjust carburetor
	Too much oil in 2-cycle fuel mix	Replace fuel with correct mix
Low power, not much smoke	Lean fuel mix	Clean or replace fuel filter. Clean or replace tank vent (usually gas cap)
Engine overheats	Cooling fins on cylinder head dirty	Clean engine. Do not get water in carburetor in process
Engine overloaded	Dull blade	Sharpen (See pages 24 to 25)

End-of-season gas-powered-tool storage

1. Perform routine maintenance service: change spark plug, check air filter, change oil (four-cycle engines).

2. Clean under deck and sharpen blade.

3. If you have been using stabilized fuel, fill the tank for storage. Warning: old unstabilized fuel can varnish and plug carburetor parts. If you have been using non-stabilized fuel, allow the engine to run until the tank runs dry. Buy new 87 octane unleaded gasoline, preferably without methane, ethane or MTBE added. Add a stabilizer according to instructions (See page 26). Fill the tank full and run the engine a little to move the fuel through the machine. If you cannot find a stabilizer, then leave the tank dry until spring after lubricating the engine (See page 27).

4. Lubricate Engine: Using an oil can, add ½ oz. (1 tablespoon) of oil through the spark plug opening. Then replace the spark plug and slowly pull the starter rope to distribute the oil (See page 27).

5. Remove the battery, if there is one, and keep it on wood in a place that stays above freezing.

6. Wipe or spray a light oil over all rust-prone parts of the machine, including blade, and cover it with a tarp.

7. Store in a dry place.

Even tools that require little or no engine maintenance should be thoroughly cleaned before off-season storage.

Creating a New Lawn

Sometimes, the best solution to a persistent yard-care problem is simply to get rid of the old grass and start fresh. With a fresh slate of dirt, you can correct any fundamental problems with the soil, provide a nutrient-rich medium for the new grass, and custom-choose a new type of grass that is perhaps better suited to your yard. Creating a new lawn is also a task many new homeowners face—look at it as an opportunity to get it right from the start.

As you begin planning a new lawn, you'll need to make two major decisions: which species of grass to plant (or which combination of species); and in what form (do you want to plant from seed, sprigs or plugs, or would you prefer to lay sod).

Grass Types

Not all grasses are created equal or can perform equally well under the diversity of conditions found from state to state or even from lawn to lawn—or even from area to area within a lawn. Different climates require different grasses, and grasses that perform well with lots of TLC may be unsuited for lawns that will receive little care. If you're planning a new lawn, this chapter can help you pick species that fit your needs and make sense for your climate.

Grasses can be divided into warm- and cool-season species. Warm-season grasses do most of their growing in the summer and usually go brown and dormant in the winter; cool-season species do best in spring and fall and may go dormant in the summer. Cool-season grasses are grown mainly in the North and warm-season grasses are grown mainly in the South. The transition zones between warm and cold weather areas generally require a mixed bag of warm-season and cool-season grasses. There are exceptions, though. Some cool-season grasses are overseeded on warm-season grasses in the South to provide green lawns in winter. Warm-season buffalograss is planted anywhere that rain is scarce, be it in the North or South. Cool-season tall fescue and Kentucky bluegrass continue to march south as improved varieties make these more popular in warm areas.

Another distinction between grass species is whether they propagate in bunches or by creeping. The *bunch grasses,* like ryegrass and the fescues, fill out by increasing in "bunches" within the same primary shoot. The *creeping grasses,* like bermudagrass, send out lateral stolons (above-ground runners) and rhizomes (below-ground runners) to create all-new, secondary shoots.

Identifying grasses. The extent to which identifying different types of grasses matters depends mostly on your level of interest in "lawnsmithing." If your goal is simply to choose an appropriate and pleasing species for your yard, being able to distinguish bentgrass from zoysiagrass may not be of critical importance. But if you have a desire to understand the plants that constitute a lawn, then learn the basic anatomy of grass plants so you can tell one from another and, at the same time, be able to identify the type of grass currently growing in your yard.

Grasses are easiest to identify by their seed heads, but this is seldom practical, since lawn grasses are usually mowed before they go to seed. In this book we identify species by characteristics of the leaf and stem.

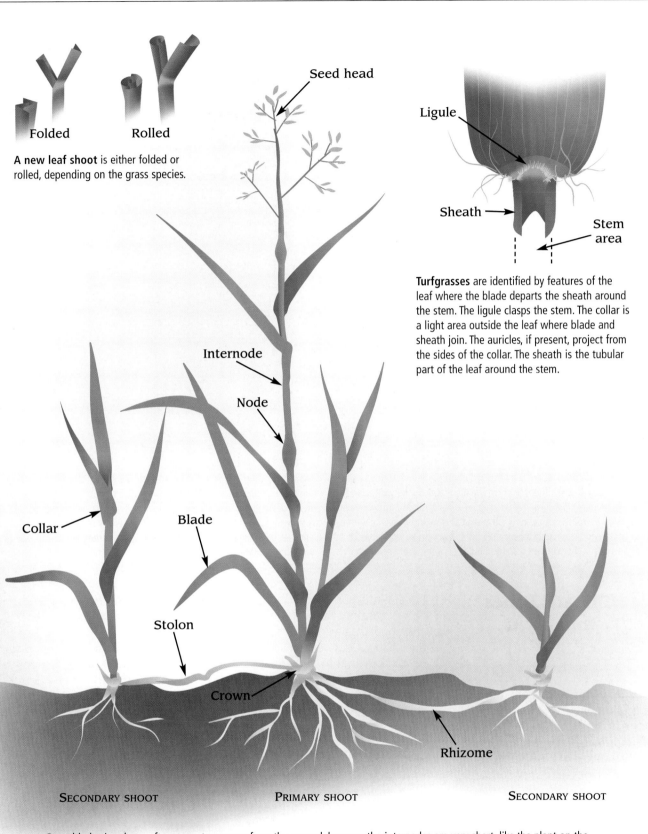

Folded   Rolled

A new leaf shoot is either folded or rolled, depending on the grass species.

Seed head

Ligule

Sheath

Stem area

Turfgrasses are identified by features of the leaf where the blade departs the sheath around the stem. The ligule clasps the stem. The collar is a light area outside the leaf where blade and sheath join. The auricles, if present, project from the sides of the collar. The sheath is the tubular part of the leaf around the stem.

Internode

Node

Collar

Blade

Stolon

Crown

Rhizome

SECONDARY SHOOT   PRIMARY SHOOT   SECONDARY SHOOT

Grass blades in a lawn often seem to emerge from the ground, because the internodes are very short, like the plant on the right. When a grass plant gets ready for reproduction, the internodes elongate and a seed head forms, as on the center plant. The little plants here did not come from seeds but from the big plant, which sent out rhizomes and stolons, a characteristic of creeping grasses like bermudagrass. Bunch grasses like ryegrass expand mainly by forming "tillers," which are new stems arising from the same crown as the mother plant.

U.S. Grass Zone Map

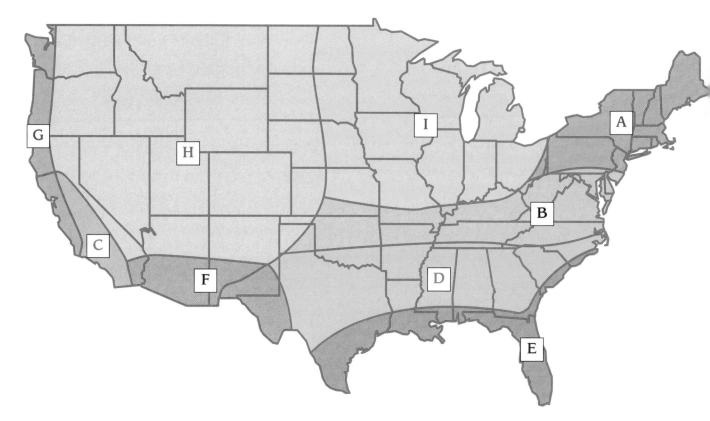

The lawn zone map above can help you figure out which grasses to grow and how to keep them healthy. The lawn zones take winter and summer temperatures into account, and also soils, rainfall patterns and wind. Keep in mind that weather patterns can vary dramatically within each zone, and your local climate may differ from the norm for your region. Typically, areas close to large bodies of water are wetter and experience more moderate temperature swings. Areas at higher elevations are colder. On a finer scale, sunny areas, south slopes, and areas south of buildings are warmer, and sandy soil and sloped land is dryer. It's always a good idea to ask a local Cooperative Extension Agent or another lawn expert for lawn-care and grass-variety advice specific to your lawn and local climate.

Climate Zones for Lawns

Northeast (A)

Cold winters and generally good precipitation allow cool-season grasses to flourish in the Northeast.

Popular lawn grasses: Cool-season mixes of bluegrasses, perennial ryegrass and the fine fescues are very common. In the coastal south of the zone, zoysiagrass (warm-season) handles summer well but will brown out in the winter.

Planting considerations: Plant from seed in August or September (after the heat breaks) so the grass has fall and spring to establish before summer heat. As a second choice, plant as soon as you can in the spring. Cool-season sods may be laid anytime from April to October, but establishment is easiest during the cool fall months. Northeast soils tend to be acid so lime may need to be added to them.

Transition Zone East (B)

What you plant depends on your local climate and what kind of lawn you want. The warm-season grasses will brown out in winter. The cool-season grasses will need a lot of water if you want them to stay green in the summer.

Popular lawn grasses: Tall fescue (cool-season), zoysiagrass (warm-season), bermudagrass (warm-season for mild winter areas).

Planting considerations: Sow cool-season grasses in September or October or early spring (less ideal). Cool-season sod can be laid any time during the growing season with enough watering, but establishment is easiest in the fall. Plant warm-season grasses from when the soil has warmed in May or June right through the summer, with earlier planting helping you avoid lots of watering and later planting helping you avoid spring weeds. Warm-season sods can be laid anytime during the growing season with adequate water.

Transition Zone West (C)

This transition zone does not get as cold as the eastern transition zone, but neither does it get very hot. For this reason, many cool-season and warm-season grasses can be grown here. Water shortages can influence grass choices in this zone.

Popular lawn grasses: Tall fescue (a cool-season grass); bermudagrass (warm-season). Overseeding with ryegrass in the winter; plant buffalograss (warm-season) for the driest areas; use drought-hardy groundcovers.

Planting considerations: Same as Transition Zone East.

Middle South (D)

The middle South has hot humid summers with good and sometimes excessive rainfall. The eastern part of the zone is wetter and the soils are more likely to be sandy, acidic and infertile. If you live in the western part of this zone, read about zones F and H too.

Popular lawn grasses: Cooler and drier parts favor tall fescue (cool-season grass) and zoysiagrass (warm-season). Warmer and wetter parts favor bermudagrass, centipedegrass and bahiagrass (all warm-season grasses). Overseed with ryegrass for winter green.

Planting considerations: Plant warm-season grasses starting April or May through the middle of the summer. Plant from sprigs, plugs or seed when the soil has warmed to at least 65°F. Plant too early and the grass becomes overrun with weeds and doesn't grow well. Plant in the heat of summer and the grass grows well but requires a lot of irrigation or rain. Lay warm-season sod in the spring, summer or early fall. Seed cool-season grasses in the fall. Lay cool-season sod in fall for best results.

Coastal Deep South (E) (includes Hawaii)

Use warm-season grasses exclusively. Lawn disease is a problem due to the wetness of the region.

Popular lawn grasses: Carpetgrass and centipedegrass (for wet, low-maintenance lawns); St. Augustinegrass, bermudagrass and zoysiagrass.

Planting considerations: Plant when the soils warms in the spring or during or just before your summer rainy season. Warm-season sods can be laid all year round in most of this zone with irrigation.

Southwest (F)

Because of water restrictions in the Southwest, many explore ways to minimize the size of lawns using drought-tolerant groundcovers.

Popular lawn grasses: Grow drought-tolerant Bermudagrass and zoysiagrass at low elevations. Overseeded bermudagrass with rye for a green winter lawn. Grow native, drought-tolerant species like buffalograss and blue gramagrass. At high elevations and in the northern part of the zone, grow natives or tall fescue blends, which stay green through the winter.

Planting considerations: Gypsum, sulfur or iron may be called for by a soil test. Cool-season grasses are best planted in March, April or early fall. Warm-season grasses can be planted in spring when the soil has warmed, which could be anytime from March to May. Plant before or during seasonal rains if possible. Contact your county Cooperative Extension Service for planting advice specific to your area.

Pacific Coastal (G)

This moderate climate favors cool-season grasses. Soils may be acid in the northern part of the zone, and could require lime.

Popular lawn grasses: The deep roots of tall fescues can carry a lawn through periods of low moisture. You may also grow bermudagrass and zoysiagrass where it is warm enough. In Oregon and Washington the bluegrasses, ryegrasses and fine fescues work well. Colonial bent-grass is popular on the northern coast also.

Planting considerations: Sow cool-season grasses in September or October or in the spring (second choice) when the ground can be worked. Lay cool-season sod March to October, with the fall being preferable, especially in warmer, dryer areas. Dry areas will require an inch per week of water when it doesn't rain, unless you want to let the grasses go dormant.

West (H)

This zone is often dry and cold.

Popular lawn grasses: Grow zoysiagrass and bermudagrass in the south, tall fescue everywhere, fine fescues and bluegrass where water is available, buffalograss where water is scarce and traffic on the lawn light.

Planting considerations: Sow cool-season grasses after the heat breaks in late summer or early fall, or as soon as you can in the spring (second best). Plant warm-season grasses from late spring to mid summer. Your soils are alkaline and salty in places, and may require special amendments like gypsum and sulfur.

Midwest (I)

This zone has generally good soils, a real winter with authentic snow, and a hot humid summer. Read also about Zone H if you live toward the west of this zone and Zone B if you live in the south.

Popular lawn grasses: Plant Kentucky bluegrass, ryegrass and fine fescues throughout; tall fescue in all but the extreme north; and zoysiagrass and bermudagrass in the lower part of the zone.

Planting considerations: Sow cool-season grasses in August or September. Sod can be laid any time during the growing season, but fall sodding makes establishment easier, since you won't need to water quite so frequently.

Bermudagrass

Bermudagrass Tip: When starting a new lawn in the fall, plant a mixture of unhulled bermudagrass seed and rye-grass. The ryegrass will cover the ground in the winter and the bermudagrass will germinate in the spring.

Zone suitability

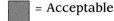

▉	= Acceptable
▉	= Borderline/risky
▉	= Not suitable

Advantages: Fine, even, rapidly spreading lawn cover; heat and drought resistant.

Disadvantages: Requires heavy watering & fertilizing and frequent mowing for optimal appearance. Does not tolerate shade. Aggressive weed in beds.

Bermudagrass, Common *(Cynodon dactylon)* and Hybrid *(Cynodon dactylon x C. transvalensis)*

Where to Plant: Prefers full sun in Zones (D), (E), (F), (C) and parts of (H) and (B). Tolerates many kinds of soil, traffic and salt.

Planting: Sow hulled common bermudagrass seed at two pounds per 1,000 sq. ft. in late spring or early summer after the soil temperature has reached at least 65°F. Mix seed thoroughly with sand for easier planting. Expect germination in 7 to 21 days, with faster germination happening between 85 and 100°. Plant 5 to 15 bushels of sprigs per 1000 sq. ft. if you broadcast, or less than a bushel if planted in rows 12 in. apart spaced 12 in. in the row. One sq. yard of sod provides about a bushel of sprigs. Plant plugs 12 in. apart.

Care:

Hybrid: Takes more care than common bermudagrass. Mow to ¾ in. with a power reel mower. Fertilize with 3 to 5 pounds of nitrogen per 1000 sq. ft. per year. Water deeply and infrequently. Use a dethatcher, a plug aerator or both if thatch buildup is excessive.

Common: Same, but power reel mower is not needed. Fertilize with 1 to 4 pounds nitrogen per 1000 sq. ft. per year.

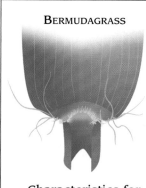

BERMUDAGRASS

Characteristics for identification:

- Leaves folded in bud
- Ligule short, hairy
- Collar narrow with long hairs
- Sheath flat
- Blades short, rough edged, sharp pointed
- Seed head 3 to 5 narrow spikes

St. Augustinegrass Tip:
Older varieties are susceptible to St. Augustine Decline (SAD) virus. Prolonged temperatures below 25°F kill St. Augustinegrass.

Advantages: A springy, luxurious grass that will tolerate shade and salt spray as long as water is ample. Recovers quickly from rough use.

Disadvantages: Does not tolerate drought, cold temperatures or disease well. High maintenance.

| A | B | C | D | E | F | G | H | I |

Zone suitability

= Acceptable

= Borderline/risky

= Not suitable

ST. AUGUSTINEGRASS

Characteristics for identification:

- Leaves folded in bud
- Ligule short, hairy
- Collar wide
- Sheath very flat
- Blade wide, short, boat shaped
- Seed head a single narrow spike

St. Augustinegrass, Common
(Stenotaphrum secundatum)

Where to Plant: Prefers the warm, wet areas of the Deep Coastal South. Will grow in southern California with enough irrigation. St. Augustinegrass is the most shade tolerant of warm-season grasses.

Planting: Plant plugs (preferable) or sprigs 6 to 12 in. apart in early spring. Requires 3 to 6 sq. yards of sod per 1000 sq. ft. if you cut your own 2-in. plugs. Requires 1 to 2 sq. yards of sod per 1000 sq. ft. if you make your own sprigs. Keep sprigs especially well watered, since St. Augustine sprigs are stolons and are less hardy than bermudagrass rhizomes.

Care: Water in the mornings to reduce disease. Fertilize in spring and fall with 2 to 5 pounds of nitrogen per 1000 sq. ft. per year. Mow to 1 to 3 in. high. High mowing discourages weeds but may encourage thatch and disease. Use a dethatcher, a plug aerator or both if thatch buildup is excessive. Test soil for iron deficiency if grass is yellowish.

Zoysiagrass

Zoysiagrass Tip: In the transition zones, zoysiagrass goes dormant early and greens up late, leaving a brown lawn while cool-season grass owners have green. It does not take well to overseeding of cool-season grasses.

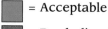

Zone suitability

◼ = Acceptable

◼ = Borderline/risky

◼ = Not suitable

Advantages: Tolerates shade, salt and high levels of traffic well; can go partly dormant in drought.

Disadvantages: Can't be planted from seed in many areas; takes a long time to establish from sprigs or plugs; spiky feel underfoot.

Zoysiagrass (*Zoysiagrass japonica, Z. matrella, Z. tenuifolia*)

Where to Plant: Broadly, zoysiagrass is planted in Zones B, C, D, E and F and southern parts of other zones where drought tolerance and some cold tolerance is desired. Zoysiagrass's cold tolerance (for a warm-season grass) makes it popular in the Eastern Transition Zone. Shade tolerance favors zoysiagrass on dry southern sites where other shade-tolerant warm-season grasses can't grow.

Planting: Sow 1 to 2 pounds of seed per 1000 sq. ft. in late spring or early summer when soil has warmed to at least 65°F. You may mix the seed thoroughly with sand to make planting easier. Plant sprigs 2 in. apart in rows 6 in. apart (3 to 6 bushels of sprigs per 1000 sq. ft.) or plugs 6 in. apart in all directions when the soil has warmed in mid to late spring. Sprigs should have one node left above the soil. Sprigs and plugs of zoysiagrass can take two years to fill in, so weed control is important. Monthly light fertilizing can help it fill in faster.

Care: After established, water zoysiagrass deeply and infrequently. Fertilize with 1 to 3 pounds of nitrogen per 1000 sq. ft. per year. Mow 1 to 2 in. high. Use a dethatcher, a plug aerator or both if thatch buildup is excessive.

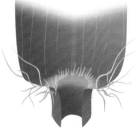

ZOYSIAGRASS

Characteristics for identification:

- Leaves rolled in bud
- Ligule hairy
- Collar with long hairs
- Blade short, pointed, stiff
- Seed head a single spike

Buffalograss Tip: Its tolerance of dry, alkaline, compacted and clay soils make it a perfect native-grass choice for low-maintenance western lawns.

Advantages: Fine blades, sod-forming, compact growth well suited for lawns; slow growing; tolerates imperfect soil conditions.

Disadvantages: Turns brown in dry summer if not watered frequently; recovers slowly from damage; seed is expensive.

A	B	C	D	E	F	G	H	I

Zone suitability

	= Acceptable
	= Borderline/risky
	= Not suitable

BUFFALOGRASS

Characteristics for identification:

- Leaves rolled in bud
- Ligule with longer hairs at sides
- Collar wide and hairy
- Blade flat, fine, dull green, sparsely hairy
- Female seed head burrs on stem above leaf collars
- Male flowers on curved branches at top

Buffalograss *(Buchloe dactyloides)*

Where to Plant: Plant this tough, warm-season native grass in full sun in the West (Zone H), the Southwest (Zone F) and other areas that receive less than 25 in. of rain a year. Buffalograss is tolerant of cold and heat extremes. Do not plant in soils that stay wet.

Planting: Sow in the late summer, early fall, or spring. Spring-planted seeds will need to be soaked and chilled first to break dormancy. Recommended seeding rates vary widely (consult your Extension Agent). Plant sprigs or plugs one foot apart. Keep watered and weeded until established.

Care: Buffalograss prefers to be left alone, as water and fertilizer favor weeds over buffalograss. Don't fertilize, or fertilize sparingly (1 pound or less of nitrogen per 1000 sq. ft. per year) in the spring. Mow to 2 or 3 in. high infrequently, or just once in the spring after the grass greens. To keep green, you may water deeply and infrequently during times of drought.

Tip: Can't find buffalograss? Blue gramagrass and western wheatgrass are two other drought-hardy low-maintenance natives more suited to some western states.

Seashore Paspalum

Seashore Paspalum Tip: Called "the environmental grass," it can be watered with pure sea water or residential waste water. If water with salts is used, the soil must be well drained so salt buildup can be flushed out with periodic heavy watering. Seashore Paspalum protects natural water supplies by filtering heavy metals from water.

Zone suitability
■ = Acceptable

■ = Borderline/risky

■ = Not suitable

Advantages: Environmentally friendly; tolerates both drought and complete submersion in water.

Disadvantages: Does not tolerate much shade or cold.

Seashore Paspalum (*Paspalum vaginatum*)

Where to Plant: Grows in the Deep Coastal South and Southern California. Tolerates high-salt, alkaline, acidic and polluted conditions.

Planting: Grow from sod or sprigs. Broadcast 5 to 14 bushels of sprigs per 1000 sq. ft. and cover thinly with soil or compost. Fertilize with 1:2:3 or 1:3:4 NPK starter fertilizer. The herbicide granular *Ronstar* is safe to use at planting.

Care: Mow ½ to 1 in. high, preferably with a sharp mulching rotary mower. Fertilize lightly with nitrogen in the fall and spring only. Fertilize with 1 to 2 pounds of potassium per 1000 sq. ft. in the fall to enhance winter hardiness.

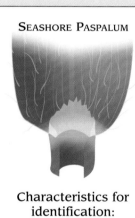

SEASHORE PASPALUM

Characteristics for identification:

- Leaves rolled in bud
- Ligule a jagged membrane
- Collar wide, hairy
- Sheath compressed
- Blade wide, prominent mid-vein
- Seed head three or more spikes

WARM-SEASON GRASSES
BAHIAGRASS *(Paspalum notatum)*

Bahiagrass prefers sun or light shade in eastern parts of the Middle South (Zone D) and in the Coastal Deep South (Zone E) but is not often found west of East Texas. Tolerates slightly acid, sandy soils but will not tolerate salt or dry, alkaline soils. Deep roots make this species good for erosion control. Bahiagrass stays green longer than most warm-season grasses in the winter and is easy to overseed with rye. It requires less fertilizer and less frequent watering than bermudagrass and St. Augustinegrass to stay green. It can be mowed high (4 in.) to control weeds, and it takes traffic well and is resistant to disease.

On the downside, bahiagrass needs fairly frequent mowing to stay looking lawn-like, and the tough leaves require a sharp blade. Though it maintains its green well, it's only moderately drought-hardy. Bahiagrass lawns appear rough. Sow seed at 7 to 10 pounds per 1,000 sq. ft. if it's scarified (preferable) and up to 14 pounds if it's not. Sow in spring and expect germination in 2 to 4 weeks. Bahiagrass may be overseeded with rye or tall fescue in the winter. Water deeply and infrequently, fertilize moderately (1 to 4 pounds nitrogen per 1000 sq. ft. per year). Mow 2 to 4 in. high.

WARM-SEASON GRASSES
CENTIPEDEGRASS *(Eremochloa ophiuroides)*

Centipedegrass prefers sun or light shade in the Middle South and Coastal Deep South (Zones D and E). It tolerates somewhat acid and poor soils, but will not tolerate salt or dry, alkaline soils. Centipedegrass is an aggressive, creeping grass resistant to chinch bugs and brown spot and a number of other diseases. It requires less mowing and fertilizer than bermudagrass. Centipedegrass is shallow-rooted and turns brown quickly in dry weather and with cold. It does not tolerate heavy traffic.

Sow seed at ¼ to 1 pound per 1,000 sq. ft. and expect germination in 20 days. Mix fine seed thoroughly with sand for easier planting. Buy 4 to 6 bushels of sprigs per 1,000 sq. ft. and plant in rows 6 in. apart, or plant plugs 6 in. apart. Keep sprigs and seed especially well watered. Plant in spring when recommended by a local Cooperative Extension Agent. The lawn will be slow to fill in.

Keep established centipedegrass watered in times of drought and fertilize lightly (1 to 2 pounds nitrogen per 1000 sq. ft. per year). Apply iron and/or sulfur (acidifier) if soil test indicates a need. This can make the grass greener, but it will never be as green as bermudagrass. Mow when needed to 1 to 2 in. high.

Rating the Warm-season Grasses

The ratings below can help you pick the grass that's right for you. For example, you can see by the chart that ryegrass is going to make a tougher play surface (through wear resistance) than bentgrass. But be aware that plant properties tend to be difficult to pin down in general terms. A species that needs a lot of additional nitrogen in one area may get by on very little in another. Note, also, that the ratings only compare species within each table. So even though zoysiagrass has a 'high' cold tolerance rating in the Warm-Season chart, it's more tender than fine fescue, which has a 'medium' rating in the Cool-Season chart.

	Bahiagrass	Bermudagrass, common	Bermudagrass, hybrid	Blue gramagrass	Buffalograss	Carpetgrass	Centipedegrass	St. Augustinegrass	Zoysiagrass
Cold Tolerance	Very low	Medium	Low	Very high	Very high	Very low	Very low	Very low	High
Drought Tolerance	Medium	High	High	Very high	Very high	Very low	Very low	Low	High
Shade Tolerance	Medium	Very low	Very low	Low	Low	Medium	Medium	Very high	High
Low "N" Tolerance	Very good	Medium	Very poor	Good	Good	Very good	Very good	Poor	Medium
Disease Resistance	Very good	Medium	Medium to good	Very good	Very good	Good	Very good	Very poor	Medium
Salt Tolerance	Very low	Very high	Very high	Good	Good	No info.	Very low	Very high	Very high
Wear Resistance	Medium	Good	Very good	Medium	Medium	Good	Very poor	Poor	Very good
Thatch Resistance	Very good	Very poor	Very poor	Very good	Very good	No Info.	Good	Poor	Poor
Establishment Rate	Medium	Very fast	Medium	Slow	Very slow	Fast	Very slow	Medium	Very slow
Recovery Rate	Fast	Very fast	Very fast	No info.	No info.	Fast	Very slow	Fast	Slow

Kentucky Bluegrass

Kentucky Bluegrass
Tip: The bluegrass family is extremely large, and includes rough bluegrass *(P. trivialis),* which tolerates shade and wet soils, but does not tolerate drought, hot sun or wear. Some newer varieties are highly disease resistant.

A	B	C	D			G	H	I

Zone suitability

- ■ = Acceptable
- ■ = Borderline/risky
- ■ = Not suitable

Advantages: Makes a fine, soft lawn with a rich green color; hundreds of varieties available.

Disadvantages: Requires a lot of water, fertilizer and mowing; does not tolerate shade; slow to germinate from seed.

Bluegrass, Kentucky *(Poa pratensis)*

Where to Plant: Plant in the sun in the northern and transitional zones (A, B, C, G, I) or in cooler parts of the South. Plant in dry western states only with ample irrigation. Kentucky bluegrass is often planted with one or more of the fine fescues, which colonize the shady and dry parts of the lawn, and perennial ryegrass, which takes over in high-wear areas.

Planting: Sow 1 to 2 pounds of seed per 1,000 sq. ft. Expect germination in 2 to 4 weeks. Kentucky bluegrass is best planted in the early fall, but early spring is a good

second choice. Sod may be planted any time during the growing season, if you can provide daily water afterward. Sod establishment is easiest in the fall.

Care: Apply 1 to 3 pounds of nitrogen per 1000 sq. ft. per year for bluegrass mixed with fescues. Water when the grass becomes dull and holds footprints, unless you want the grass to go dormant. Mow to 1½ to 3 in. high, using the greater height to suppress spring weeds and to carry the lawn through drought and hot summer weather.

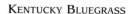

KENTUCKY BLUEGRASS

Characteristics for identification:

- Leaves folded in bud
- Ligule a short membrane
- Collar narrow
- Sheath green, flattened
- Blades long, narrow, with boat-shaped tip
- Seed head branched and open, like a conifer tree

Ryegrass Tip: New varieties of perennial ryegrass are less coarse and shaggy than their ancestors. Many varieties have endophytes against insects.

Advantages: Quick germination, fast establishment, and endurance under traffic make it popular on well-used lawns.

Disadvantages: Does not tolerate deep shade or extreme cold or heat.

| A | B | C | D | E | F | G | H | I |

Zone suitability

- = Acceptable
- = Borderline/risky
- = Not suitable

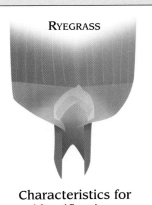

RYEGRASS

Characteristics for identification:

- Leaves folded in bud
- Ligule a long membrane
- Collar narrow
- Blades clearly veined
- Seed head a spike bearing short spikelets along length

Ryegrass, Perennial *(Lolium perenne)*

Where to Plant: Plant alone or mixed with bluegrass and fescues in all northern zones in areas that receive heavy traffic. Use also where quick cover is desired. Use to overseed southern lawns for winter green.

Planting: Sow at rates recommended for individual varieties, usually 4 to 8 pounds of seed per 1000 sq. ft. When overseeding, spread at double the rate for cleared ground.

Care: Mow 2 to 3 in. high, using the greater height to suppress weed competition in the spring or to help the lawn stay green during drought. Fertilize with 1 to 3 pounds of nitrogen per 1000 sq. ft. per year. High-maintenance lawns with very long growing seasons may need more fertilizer. Water regularly.

Related Species: Annual ryegrass *(L. multiflorum)* is also used for annual overseeding in the South. It grows quickly but dies after one year. Northern mixes should contain little or no annual rye.

Tall Fescue

Tall Fescue Tip: Tall fescue is tough underfoot, making it useful for athletic fields and play areas.

A B C D E F G H I

■ = Acceptable

▨ = Borderline/risky

■ = Not suitable

Advantages: Great wearability and low fertilizer need; tolerant of shade, disease and drought.

Disadvantages: Intolerant of humid, wet heat; relatively coarse.

Fescue, Tall *(Festuca arundinaciea)*

Where to Plant: Deep-rooted tall fescue is tolerant of warm, dry climates in sun and shade. Grow in Zones B, C and F; in the dryer parts of Zone D; and in warmer parts of Zone H. Tall fescue is used to overseed southern lawns for winter green.

Planting: Look for blends of two or more cultivars. Sow 4 to 10 pounds of tall fescue seed per 1000 sq. ft., depending on variety. It should germinate in 7 to 12 days. Plant in the early fall or early spring. Tall fescue may also be purchased as sod.

Care: Apply 1 to 4 pounds of nitrogen per 1000 sq. ft. per year using the higher rate when the grass is irrigated over a long growing season. Mow 2 to 3 in. high, using the greater height for suppressing weeds, for drought conditions and for shady sites. Water infrequently and deeply.

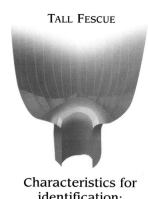

TALL FESCUE

Characteristics for identification:

- Leaves folded in bud
- Ligule a short membrane
- Collar narrow
- Sheath green, flattened
- Blades long, narrow, with boat-shaped tip
- Seed head branched and open, like a conifer tree

Fine Fescue Tip:
The other fine fescues are bunch grasses and are more tolerant of heat than red fescue. Sheep fescue *(F. ovina)* is good for out-of-the-way, dry and shady nooks with little traffic. Hard fescue *(F. longifolia)* is well suited for stabilizing banks under dry conditions at high elevations. Chewings fescue *(F. rubra commutata)* can tolerate poor acidic soil and is fast-growing enough to compete with weeds in the shade.

Advantages: Does well in shade; thin, fine texture.

Disadvantages: Does not wear well; susceptible to disease; does poorly in high heat.

A	B	C	D	E	F	G	H	I

Zone suitability

☐ = Acceptable

☐ = Borderline/risky

☐ = Not suitable

Fescue, Red *(Festuca rubra)*

RED FESCUE

Characteristics for identification:

- Leaves folded in bud
- Ligule a short membrane
- Collar narrow
- Sheath round and wider than blade
- Blade very narrow
- Seed head narrowly branched with spikelets

Where to Plant: Red fescue is the most widely planted fine fescue. Plant with bluegrass to colonize dry and shady parts of the lawn. Red fescue is sometimes used on slopes in pure stands, where it can be mowed for a lawn or left unmown for an attractive groundcover effect. Red fescue is used most around the Great Lakes, in the Northeast, and in the Pacific Northwest. In contrast to other fine fescues, red fescue is a creeping grass and is considered the most refined.

Planting: When planted alone, sow 3 to 5 pounds of seed per 1000 sq. ft. Follow seeding recommendations for blends. Expect germination in 1 to 3 weeks. In the North, the fine fescues are best planted in the early fall or the cool part of spring.

Care: The fine fescues suffer from disease and weed competition if watered and fertilized too much. In the fall, apply compost or 1 to 2 pounds slow-release nitrogen per 1000 sq. ft. Water infrequently but deeply. Mow 2 to 3 in. high. Use the greater height in shade; when annual weeds are germinating in the spring; and before, during and after drought.

Bentgrass

Colonial Bentgrass
Tip: In damp parts of the Pacific Northwest, you may grow colonial bentgrass without much fertilizer and care, especially if you see your neighbors growing it successfully or are advised to grow it by a local expert.

| A | B | C | D | E | F | G | H | I |

Zone suitability (Colonial)

■ = Acceptable

▨ = Borderline/risky

■ = Not suitable

Advantages: Colonial variety is an attractive, tight-knit sod that makes a nice, even lawn surface.

Disadvantages: Colonial damages easily and is fairly high maintenance; creeping is very high maintenance and not recommended for homes.

Bentgrass, Colonial *(Agrostis tenuis)* and Creeping *(A. stolonifera)* (shown above)

Where to Plant: Colonial bentgrass is well adapted to full sun or light shade in the Pacific Northwest, but is very difficult to grow anywhere else. In the Northwest it coexists with various bluegrasses and weed grasses. Creeping bentgrass is very high maintenance and is only appropriate on putting greens, lawn bowling greens, grass tennis courts and the like.

Planting (Colonial): Sow ½ to 2 pounds of colonial bentgrass seed per 1000 sq. ft. and expect germination in 1 to 3 weeks, or plant plugs according to your supplier's instructions. Seed is usually sown in the early spring.

Care: In naturally damp and cool areas, apply compost or 1 or 2 pounds of slow-release nitrogen per 1000 sq. ft. per year, in the fall. Where the grass is irrigated over a long season, apply 4 pounds or more of nitrogen per 1000 sq. ft., distributed in 1-pound doses in fall and spring. Bentgrass needs frequent irrigation to stay green if rain and fog is insufficient, or it may be allowed to go dormant. Aerate and dethatch annually if needed. Mow colonial bentgrass ½ to 1 in. high.

CREEPING BENTGRASS

Characteristics for identification:

- Leaves rolled in bud
- Ligule a tall membrane
- Collar narrow
- Sheath round
- Blade narrow and veined
- Seed head narrowly branched with spikelets

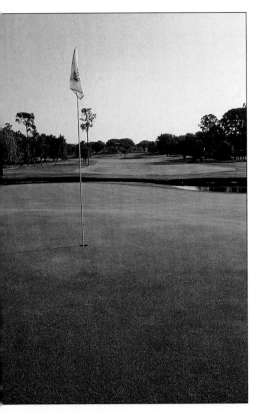

Creeping bentgrass is the most-often-used grass for golf course putting greens. It is a beautiful but high-maintenance grass that is better avoided in residential yards.

The Ecolawn

Oregon turf scientist Tom Cook was after the perfect lawn—one that would require no fertilizer, little water and infrequent mowing. Cook soon realized that grass alone wasn't going to cut it, so he turned from the American concept of "lawn" to the medieval concept of "flowery mead," a sward of grasses and other low-growing flowering plants developed in Europe for the recreation of lords and ladies. After years of research the *Ecolawn* was born, a combination of grasses, clover, yarrow, English daisies and chamomile.

The *Ecolawn* is low, drought tolerant and a delight to look at and walk barefoot upon. While the *Ecolawn* itself is available from Nichols Garden Nursery in Albany, Oregon, Cook encourages lawn growers everywhere to not worry too much about "weeds" but allow the toughest, best adapted grasses and plants to step up to the plate for a durable, low-maintenance groundcover. "A good lawn," says Cook, "is one that looks good from across the street."

Cool-season Grasses (values relative to species within table only)

	Bentgrass, colonial	Bentgrass, creeping	Bluegrass, Kentucky	Fescue, fine (including red, hard, sheep and chewings)	Fescue, tall	Ryegrass, perennial
Heat Tolerance	Low	High	Medium	Medium	Very high	Low
Cold Tolerance	High	Very high	High	Medium	Medium	Medium
Drought Tolerance	Very low	Very low	Medium	High	High	Low
Shade Tolerance	Medium	Medium	Low	Very high	High	Medium
Low "N" Tolerance	Usually poor	Very poor	Poor	Very good	Good	Poor
Disease Resistance	Poor	Very poor	Good	Medium	Very good	Medium
Salt Tolerance	Very low	Good	Low	Low	Good	Medium
Wear Resistance	Low	Low	Medium	Low-medium	Very good	Good
Thatch Resistance	Poor	Very poor	Medium	Medium	Good	Good
Establishment Rate (from seed)	Medium	Medium	Very slow	Fast	Fast	Very fast
Recovery Rate	No info.	Very fast	Very fast	Very slow	Fast	Fast

Plant seeds (pages 58 to 63)

Plant sprigs (pages 64 to 65)

Plant plugs (page 66)

Lay sod (pages 67 to 69)

Preparing Your Yard for Planting

Planting grass is a relatively easy, even satisfying experience, provided you approach it with attention and patience. Attention means you don't plant a lawn before your two-week vacation, and patience means a willingness to water and wait—sometimes up to a month after planting—for the grass seedlings to make their appearance.

Before you begin to prepare the soil and make your planting decisions, it's always a good idea to get advice from your local County Extension Agent (you can find contact information located in the "County" section of the phone directory under the headings "Cooperative Extension Service" or possibly "Extension"). Also,

be sure to read about your grass zone (See pages 34 to 35) before you choose a species of grass plant and the optimal planting time. As you devise your new lawn planting schedule, be sure to allow about a month to take care of any bad weed or creeping grass problem, since they may continue to sprout from seed, root and rhizome for some time after your initial attack. This is especially true if you have creeping perennial weeds like bermudagrass or bindweed. If you're getting professional help with irrigation, grading, drainage or breaking up hardpan, line up the contractors twice as far in advance as you think you need to. Finally, make sure you have prepared for that first critical month in the life of a new lawn. Whether you lay sod or plant from seed, sprigs or plugs, you'll need to make sure that watering occurs every day, sometimes even multiple times in a day.

New-lawn Planting Checklist

- ✔ Assess the soil conditions
- ✔ Clear or kill weeds and old grass
- ✔ Grade and improve drainage, if needed
- ✔ Measure and record square footage of yard
- ✔ Amend and fertilize the soil
- ✔ Till or roughen ground
- ✔ Set up a watering system (soaker hoses, sprinklers or underground sprinkler system)
- ✔ Plant appropriate grass species
- ✔ Water and fertilize on a schedule

Measure the area of your yard you intend to plant to determine its total square footage. You may need to break the yard into several areas, calculate the square footage of each area, then tally up the total. You'll need to know the precise total square footage to correctly estimate how much planting material, fertilizer and other amendments you will need, as well as for ongoing maintenance of your lawn.

Evaluating your yard & planting conditions

Start a "Lawn and Garden" folder and keep it with your household files; this is where you'll keep a record of everything you do with your lawn and garden. Your first entries may include the soil test results, the dimensions and square footage of your lawn, planting dates and grass varieties used, fertilizing dates and quantities/types of fertilizer used.

Soil Testing. If your previous lawn suffered from spareness, weediness or disease, or if you are planting a brand-new lawn, you should get a soil test. Your best option for testing is to have it done professionally by your local Cooperative Extension Service (NOTE: In California and Illinois you will need to use a private soil lab). When you send the samples, request recommended spreading rates of soil amendments for the kinds of plants or grass you are trying to grow. Be sure to indicate where the samples came from, whether you've added anything to the soil, and, if so, when you added it. Typically, they'll test for texture, pH, phosphorous, potassium and organic matter. They may recommend testing for special problems depending on your area and situation.

To prepare a soil sample for testing, dig four or five small holes about 6 in. deep around the yard, saving the sod plug and avoiding areas where contamination is likely (for example, right next to buildings or near an outdoor grill). Take a ½-in. slice of soil from the side of

Soil testing. Collect soil from several areas in your yard and blend them together to provide the soil testing facility with a sample that's representative of your whole yard. See the discussion to the left for more information on obtaining a soil test.

each hole—the top 3 in. are most important for established lawns and the top 6 in. are most important for areas where the soil will likely be turned and amended. Before adding each sample to the bucket, cut off the top ½ in., which may be contaminated with animal urine or other surface substances. Replace unused soil in the hole and replace the sod plug. Mix all the samples together well, then place about a pint from the mixture into a clean plastic bag or container. Deliver the sample to the testing facility as directed.

Clear old grass & weeds

Before your yard is ready for "in with the new," it needs to experience "out with the old." That means killing all the old grass and weeds. There are several methods for doing this, as you'll see here. Whichever you choose, allow at least a month for this phase of your new lawn project.

Method 1: Spray Herbicide

Advantages: Kills the plants to the roots. Little physical work. Perfect for starting a northern lawn in the fall or southern lawn in the early summer.

Disadvantages: Prepares ground too late in the spring for starting a northern lawn, if spring seeding is desired. Will not kill weed seeds.

How to: The plant-killer glyphosate (Roundup, Kleenup) may be used once or twice over a period of weeks to eliminate old grass and weeds. The best temperature for applying is between 60 and 85°F. Don't mow the area for a couple of weeks before spraying to let the weeds and grass get big, so they will have plenty of leaf area to absorb the herbicide, and water the soil 6 in. deep a couple of days in advance of spraying to make sure the weeds are really growing well—the more active they are, the better they'll absorb the herbicide. Apply the herbicide according to instructions with a pump sprayer or backpack sprayer. Read all directions and cautions. Water again two or three days after applying glyphosate, if conditions are still dry.

If you have tough, creeping perennial weeds, like bermudagrass or bindweed, that don't die after a week, wait two weeks from the first application, then spray again. This waiting period allows the weeds to

Spray herbicides need to handled with caution, and the product manufacturer's application instructions must be followed to the letter. But of all the methods of killing off a problem yard, it is the least labor intensive and, arguably, the most effective.

recover and begin growing again. Water two or three days after applying the herbicide. After the weeds are truly dead, wait the recommended amount of time on the glyphosate formulation you've used before planting. Usually a day or two is sufficient.

GLYPHOSATE

Area treated with glyphosate

Untreated area

Glyphosate is the most common general herbicide for lawn grasses and weeds. When applied under the right conditions, it kills all of the vegetation it contacts. You may have to reapply on tough creeping grasses two weeks after an initial spraying.

Killing crabgrass

Crabgrass grows from a seed bank in the soil, and will not be controlled by glyphosate or weed removal. You may use a selective preemergent herbicide if you have identified crabgrass in your old lawn or former weed patch. Siduron *(Tupesan)* and simazine *(Princep)* prevent germination of crabgrass. These selective, preemergent herbicides may be applied directly after seeding or sprigging and rolling, since the appropriate chemical will not inhibit germination and growth of non-target species. Remember, preemergent herbicides will not kill crabgrass that has already sprouted, so make sure no weeds are growing when you seed and apply the herbicide. Furthermore, do not disturb the soil at all after applying any preemergent, or effectiveness will be lost.

Use siduron when planting the cool-season grasses, except bentgrass. Zoysiagrass, except for *Zoysia tenuifolia*, is the only warm-season genus that tolerates siduron. Use simazine only when planting sprigs or plugs of bermudagrass, centipedegrass, St. Augustinegrass and all zoysiagrasses (except *Z. tenuifolia*, which is non-tolerant). Do not use simazine with any grass planted from seed or with any non-tolerant species.

See pages 36 to 46 to identify grass types, and page 104 for crabgrass identification help.

Method 2: Solarization

Advantages: Kills plants and seeds.

Disadvantages: Requires direct, hot sunlight in the summer to work, which can affect timing of planting.

How to: If you can, do soil amending, tillage and grading before solarizing. This provides an even, dark surface that absorbs the heat of the sun and offers no pockets of protection for the seeds, roots and rhizomes of weeds. Also, you won't bring fresh, unburnt seeds up from underground before planting, which you would do if you turned the soil after solarizing. Spread clear plastic over the area, overlapping the edges and holding the plastic in place with boards, rocks or dirt. Clear plastic left in place two weeks to a month in hot weather will kill roots and weed seeds that are near the surface. To solarize an area without turning the soil, mow everything low and water the ground well before spreading the plastic in place.

Method 3: Removing Old Grass & Weeds

Advantages: No waiting.

Disadvantages: Requires the most work. May require loss of organic matter and topsoil from lawn as you attempt to remove living weed parts. Some living roots, rhizomes and seeds inevitably escape.

How to: If you are not trying to eliminate creeping grasses and perennial weeds, simply till the soil and rake out visible chunks of plant material. For grasses and weeds with lots of rhizomes, rent a sod kicker and peel off the top inch or two of soil. Pile this material upside down in a square compost pile with a depression on top to collect water. It will rot in less than a year. Use resulting soil/compost to topdress the lawn.

A large tiller is well worth the rental price if you're turning up a large section of yard for weed removal.

After tilling, rake out all clumps of organic matter with a garden rake. The best way to get rid of the debris is to compost it.

Grading Basics

Warning: Before digging on your property, call your local gas utility and get the public number to call to alert all underground services in your area. Each is required to mark your property to indicate the locations of pipes and wires (although, in most cases a single field agent will mark all utilities at once).

Before planting or renovating lawns or landscapes, grading and drainage problems need to be addressed. Grading concerns the shape and slope of your property, while drainage concerns the path water takes when it rains. Re-grading an area can mitigate drainage problems that are the result of poor grading. If your problems are serious, consulting a landscaping contractor could save you money and time in the long run.

TIP: Water from drain spouts should be directed away from the house with a long splash block. Alternatively, slope an underground, corrugated-plastic tube from the downspout to a swale or to a dry well (See "Drainage Basics" in this chapter).

1 Add soil if necessary. Ideally, you should have at least 6 in. of drop in the first 10 ft. away from your foundation. Do not pile dirt against wood trim, siding or window frames though. Metal basement window wells can be purchased at home centers if you need to pile soil higher on the foundation than your basement windowsills allow. Tamp or roll soil a little as you go if you are adding a lot.

2 Grade with a rake. After piling soil, use a simple iron garden rake or a landscaping rake to smooth and shape the soil. You can use the rake tines to move larger amounts of soil, or turn the rake upside down and use the back of the rake at a low angle to get a smooth soil surface.

Tip: Some people will drag a large board or a ladder with ropes tied to each end across an area they want to get flat. However you do it, your goal is to remove dips and hills and get the overall slope you want.

3 Keep soil below the surface levels of patios, walks and driveways. These surfaces should drain onto the grass or planting beds, not the other way around. Also, avoid sloping a lawn or bed steeply toward pavement. After rolling or tamping, you should have a slight lip of exposed stone or concrete on the sides of pavement. This lip acts as an edge. Leave a higher lip next to garden beds to hold back mulch and loose dirt. Some landscapers will dig trenches 1 ft. wide and 3 ft. deep along problem patios, walks and drives and fill these with gravel to receive runoff.

4 Roll, tamp or water and rake again. For lawns, you want your soil soft, but not too fluffy in texture. Your foot should sink into a properly compacted lawn bed no more than ½ in. A good rain or a sprinkling can help settle a soil, but you'll have to wait a day or more before the bed is dry enough to re-grade it with a rake or board. A half-filled lawn roller or a hand tamper will pat down a lawn bed about the right amount, but then you will want to rake it or drag it again since it will compress unevenly. Sometimes repeated rolling and raking is needed to achieve a stable, even surface. A final raking, after the last rolling, is needed to rough up the soil to receive seed or sod. For a garden bed, rolling is generally unnecessary. You're ready for planting after grading the first time.

Fill a rented lawn roller only half-full with water when compacting new or freshly turned soil for a lawn bed.

Drainage Basics

Common residential drainage systems employ swales, drainage pipe, drainage tile and dry wells. Subsoil treatments—including subsoil chisel plowing, slicing and ripping—allow water and air to get past compacted impervious layers below the topsoil. Most drainage projects should be contracted out to landscape professionals, since they require heavy machinery that's difficult to operate. Below are some examples of drainage solutions that could be helpful in your yard.

Subsoiling

If parts of your lawn stay wet too long, you may have a compacted layer under the topsoil called *hardpan* or *caliche*. This is a different problem than compacted topsoil, which calls for aeration and organic matter. Try driving a metal rod into your yard in different places. If it always meets heavy resistance at the same level, look for someone with a subsoiler or chisel plow in the phone directory under "Lawn and Grounds Maintenance." Small farmers may also have appropriate subsoiling equipment for hire.

Test for hardpan in the subsoil by driving a metal rod into the ground in several spots within lawn areas that show signs of poor drainage. If, while driving the rod, you meet resistance at a near-uniform depth throughout the problem area, the chances are good that you've got a layer of hardpan under the lawn. To remedy the problem, hire a landscape contractor to chisel plow the area, breaking up the hardpan.

IMPROVING DRAINAGE:
Drainage Swales

Swales are shallow ditches commonly used to drain lawns. They can also be used to carry water away from depressions near the house. The curving sides and bottoms of swales should be gradual enough for easy mowing. If swales do not maintain a consistent downward slope along their lengths, they can become swampy and require attention. Landscape contractors either reshape problem swales, or they bury drainage tile beneath the swale.

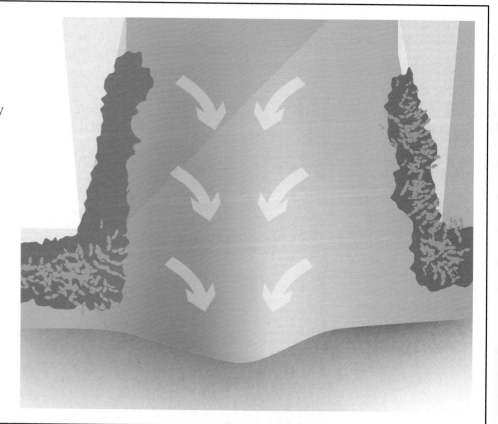

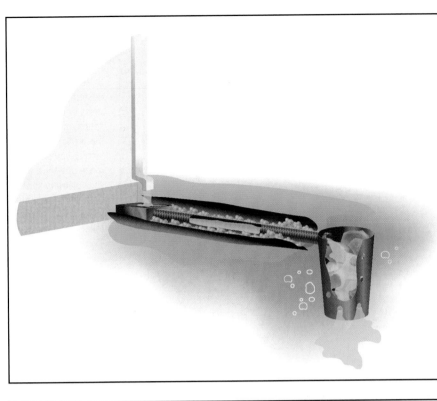

Dry Wells

Dry wells, also called *French drains,* are underground caverns filled with rocks used to disperse water into the subsoil. Have dry wells installed to receive water from downspouts, outdoor sinks and spigots, or even sinks and showers in vacation cabins (check with local authorities on rules regarding waste water disposal). In some areas, dry wells are used to address poorly drained soils. This works best when an impermeable layer of clay overlies a well-drained layer of sand or gravel. Dry wells are usually placed at least 10 ft. away from foundation walls. They will not be effective if the water table is very high.

Drain Tile

Modern drain tile is usually flexible, corrugated plastic pipe with holes on the bottom to let water in and out. Tile is buried behind retaining walls, next to house foundations, beneath damp dips in a lawn, and in any other place where underground water needs to be collected and carried away. Tile can also be used to bleed water from drain spouts into the soil, to the benefit of trees, shrubs and other deep-rooted plants.

Drain tile should be laid onto a gravel base, then covered with additional gravel to increase the flow rate of water into and out of the tile. The gravel should be wrapped with permeable landscaping fabric to help repel roots and to keep the gravel from becoming clogged with dirt.

The tile itself needs to slope consistently to an above-ground outlet or dry well. The upstream end of a tile may come to the surface in an elevated catch basin or as a capped access for putting root killer down the tile.

Add compost. With or without a soil test, it almost invariably helps your new yard to add compost, composted manure, peat moss or some other source of organic matter to your soil. Ideally, you should make one-third of your planting soil organic matter: that means, if you'll be tilling to a 6-in. depth, you'll add a 2-in. layer of organic matter.

Amending & Fertilizing Soil

Apply any amendments called for by your soil test (See page 49). Rock phosphate, lime, sulfur, gypsum or potassium compounds should be added before tillage, at the rate recommended by the soil lab—but only if called for by a soil test. Adding inorganic minerals and some fertilizers that are not needed usually does more harm than good. However, it's okay to use a complete fertilizer, such as a lawn-starter fertilizer, without a soil test, since these just add enough minerals for the immediate needs of the sprouting plants. As a general rule, apply enough of the starter fertilizer to add one pound of nitrogen per 1000 sq. ft. for lawns and other plantings.

High-carbon, organic materials need nitrogen to decompose. If you're using a high-carbon material, like sawdust, add an extra pound of nitrogen for every half-cubic-yard of material. For example, you would add 10 pounds of a fertilizer that is 10% nitrogen ("10" is the first of three numbers prominently displayed on the bag) to half a yard of partially rotted sawdust. If you are purchasing the organic material from a garden supply store, check to find out if nitrogen has already been added.

TIP: Your ability to turn fibrous organic matter into your soil depends on the size and power of your tillage equipment. After a little experimentation, you may find you need to remove excessive amounts of dead top-growth and compost it separately. Determine this before you leave the chopped-down matter in the soil and bury it with compost and other amendments.

Estimating Quantities

Bulk materials like soil, compost and manure are usually sold by the cubic yard. A cubic yard is $3 \times 3 \times 3 = 27$ cubic feet. For example, if you want to add 2 in. of composted manure to a future lawn area that is 400 sq. ft. in area, you will first divide 400 by 6, since that's how many square feet of ground a cubic foot of soil will cover when spread 2 in. thick. Divide this new number by 27, to arrive at the number of yards of manure you will need delivered. In this case, about 2.5 yards (roughly a full-size pickup load).

Tilling

Tilling the soil is no longer an automatic part of planting a lawn or groundcovers. A low-mowed stubble of herbicide-killed grass and weeds, left in place, can prevent soil runoff on slopes—a likely occurrence if you till the soil. Tilling can also stir up weed seeds that would otherwise remain buried and dormant. Fertilizers and compost may still be used on untilled soils, though generally in reduced quantities.

Tilling does have its uses, however, and is often necessary for establishing healthy new plants. Tillage is advisable when planting sod or sprigs. Tilling introduces air and can mix organic matter into hard compacted soils. In areas that suffer from hard clay soils, Extension Agents almost invariably advise tillage for planting lawns. Tilling permits the incorporation of soil conditioners and amendments in quantities recommended by a soil test. In particular, if your soil test calls for sulfur or lime to adjust a pH problem, these are best tilled in. If you add more than ½ in. of compost or if you add new soil, these should be tilled in to prevent layering. Finally, tilling turns the soil from a solid to a semi-fluid, which can be raked, smoothed, shaped, easily scooped to set plants, or scratched and pushed to lightly bury seeds.

In rural areas, you may be able to get your yard plowed, disked and harrowed by a local farmer. Otherwise, rent or borrow a rear-tine rototiller. If your yard is at all typical, you'll want the heaviest machine you can find. Avoid tillers with the tines in the front, as these are better for previously worked gardens. Sometimes you can rent a small garden tractor with a tiller attachment.

Water dry areas thoroughly at least two days before tilling to soften the soil. When it comes time to till, you want the soil soft but not wet. If a handful of soil can be molded into a moist lump that sticks together or if your soil sticks to a shovel, it's too wet for tilling and you risk damaging your soil structure by doing so.

Rent a heavy-duty tiller with the tines in the rear, not in front, to turn and mix soil for a new lawn bed.

Luckily, you're not likely to get it to this point with a sprinkler. Sod does not generally need to be stripped from the ground before tilling if it has been killed with glyphosate. When you do till, do not overdo it; leave plenty of marble and golf-ball size chunks in the soil. Whipping the soil into a fluff encourages uneven settling of a lawn and loss of organic matter to oxidation. After tilling, you need to rake out debris that would get in the way of planting and then grade the soil.

Watering a new lawn

Make sure you have sprinklers, hoses or an in-ground system on hand before you do your planting. A new lawn must be watered regularly. For the first month after planting, a seeded lawn must be watered multiple times every day. This also means someone should be available over the course of the first month to turn the sprinklers on and off. A programmable watering timer can substitute for some of that human attention.

Grass seed can be purchased in bulk or in bags. Although many hardware stores and building centers stock grass seed, your best chance for getting fresh product is at a local nursery or garden center.

Planting a Lawn from Seed

Planting from seed offers several advantages over planting sprigs or plugs or laying sod. Most notably, seed is cheaper. Plus, if you plant from seed you'll usually find a greater selection of grass species and variety options, especially in the North. Also, if you wish to expand your scope of lawn expertise, a lawn grown from seed is a hands-on lesson that will yield maximum satisfaction for the curious do-it-yourselfer.

When to plant

A lawn should be seeded immediately before the period most favorable to the growth of the species of grass you're planting. The cool-season grasses do most of their growing in the fall and spring. Therefore, planting in early fall or late summer is perfect, since the grass has warm soil to germinate in, followed by two full seasons to develop roots before the heat of the next summer. Early spring is a passable second choice for sowing cool-season grasses, but you'll encounter more weed competition for the grass.

Warm-season grasses do most of their growing when it's hot. In most cases, these should be seeded in the spring or early summer, when night temperatures rise to around 65°, but before the real heat of summer has arrived. If you plant warm-season grasses earlier than this, they may be overrun with a flush of spring weeds.

You can plant warm-season grasses through midsummer if irrigation is sufficient, but you must not let the plants dry out completely until they've established strong roots, which can be a month for slow germinators like buffalograss. This may mean watering three or four times a day. If you have a summer rainy season, plan to be ready to plant just before this to cut down on watering.

The importance of soil temperature. In the southern half of the U.S., warm-season grass seed is best planted when the soil temperature is just right. If you poke a soil thermometer (an inexpensive item sold at most nurseries or garden centers) into the ground between 10 and 11 o'clock in the morning, it should read at least 65°F; this lets you know the soil is warm enough for the warm-season grass seed to germinate.

While you can plant warm-season grasses fairly late in the summer and into the fall in far southern areas, bear in mind the importance of getting good grass establishment before winter. The warm-season grasses will slow down when the temperatures and light levels drop in the fall, and you may be contending with cool-season weeds as well. There are variations in acceptable planting times that depend on where you live and when the weeds are germinating in your area. See the description of your grass climate zone (beginning on page 34) for the best times to plant, and, as always, contact your county Cooperative Extension Service for advice.

Buying seed

Before buying your grass seed, read about grasses and your grass zone (See pages 34 to 47). Also observe how much sun and rain your yard gets, and evaluate your soil conditions, preferably with the help of experts.

Once you've selected a variety of seed, be it a single species or blend, purchase the highest quality seed available. Seed is cheap in the grand scale of things, so don't hesitate to spend more for good seed from a garden center or a mail-order seed company. It will save you money and time in the long run. Buy trade-named varieties. Seed that's labeled simply "Kentucky bluegrass" instead of, for example, "Adelphi Kentucky bluegrass," may be an unimproved product. If you see "VNS" on the seed bag label, avoid it: this means "variety not stated." It's better to choose improved varieties that specifically address your needs. If your last lawn suffered from a disease or insect problem, do your best to identify the pest or pathogen, and find an improved species or variety with resistance to that organism.

When purchasing seed, examine the label of the product you're considering for germination percentages. Germination percentages should be at least 75% for Kentucky bluegrass and 85% for others. Buy seed packed for the current growing season. Leftover seed will have reduced germination. Annual grasses should be less than 5% nongerminating, since these die after one season. Avoid seeds with any percentage of "nox-

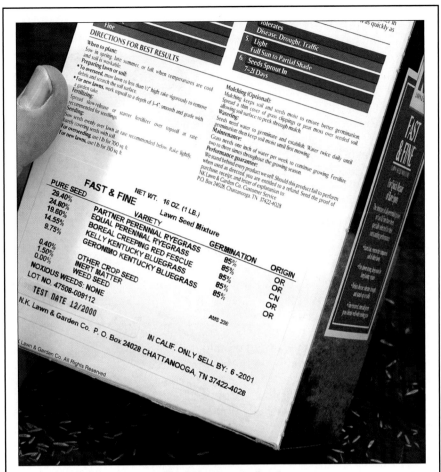

Read the label

The label on bagged or boxed grass seed should provide most of the information you need to make a good seed-purchasing decision. For example, it will tell you whether the seed is a straight, single-variety product, a blend of two or more varieties of the same species, or a mixture of two or more species (mixtures are common in cool-season lawns in the North). It will list a packaged-on or use-by date (buy seed that was packed for the current growing season), and should also list a germination percentage, along with specific variety information, including any improvements made to the variety. If any of this information is missing, look for another product. You don't want to take the chance of getting poor-performing seed.

ious" weeds. Other weed and crop seeds should constitute no more than 1 or 2% of the product. Watch out for species you don't recognize and that don't have a variety name—they may be weed grasses. Finally, bring along a calculator and the square footage of your lawn, so you know how much to buy. Buy a little extra to keep in the refrigerator in case some areas don't take.

TIP: Record species and variety information for future reference. This will allow you to patch the lawn with the same kinds of grass. This is particularly important for warm-season grasses in the South, where different species will segregate into distinct patches rather than blend harmoniously.

Sowing Seed

Before actually planting your grass seed, run through the checklist on page 48 to make sure you haven't left out any preparation and that your soil is ready for seed. Note that a tilled lawn bed should exhibit footprints no more than ½ in. deep when stepped upon, and that it should be roughened with a rake just prior to seeding. An untilled bed should have roughened, exposed soil to receive the seed, even if some of the old dead grass remains.

Use a broadcast spreader or drop spreader to distribute your seed, employing the "two batch" method of seeding illustrated here. With a drop spreader, you want to overrun the wheel tracks to get even coverage. Shut off the flow of seed when you pass over finished edge strips. Lay only the recommended quantity of seed—too much leads to overcrowded, weak plants; too little leads to a lawn that fills in slowly and will not compete well with weeds.

Spread a thin layer of fine compost or topsoil (no more than ¼ in.) over the seeded ground, using a peat spreader or just your hands. Alternatively, rake the seed in and cover it with straw to reduce moisture loss. One bale of straw will cover about 1000 square feet. Whichever method you use, roll the area with an empty or partially filled roller to press the soil into contact with the seed.

1 Do the math and set apart the amount of seed you need for your planting area. Divide the total amount you plan to spread in half. Calibrate a broadcast or drop spreader to half of the recommended spreading rate (unless it's mixed with sand) and put in half your seed.

2 Spread the edges of the planting area first, then do the middle, leaving a slight overlap between runs. Put the rest of the seed in the hopper, do the edges again then spread the middle in a pattern perpendicular to the first. This helps ensure even seed distribution.

3 Rake soil lightly to cover most, but not all, of the seed, and spread weed-free straw so that about 25% of the soil still shows through. This will keep the soil moist and help protect the seed from hungry birds, but will not interfere with the growing grass.

Aftercare of a seeded lawn

Once the grass seed is spread, apply an inch of water to the entire seeded area (use straight-sided cans as gauges—See page 76). Avoid puddling and runoff, which can displace the seed. If necessary, apply the water with several five or ten-minute sprinklings. After this initial deep watering, water shallowly once, twice or three times daily, depending on the grass species, air temperature and precipitation. Continue sprinkling at this rate until the seeds germinate. You want the soil to stay moist, but not become saturated, since overly wet soil encourages disease. Germinating seed will die in dry soil.

After germination, reduce the frequency of watering and increase the amount of water applied at each application until you achieve a regular schedule, in which the soil is allowed to dry to 6 in. or more before a deep watering (See page 76 for more information on watering). By allowing the soil to dry between waterings, you encourage deep rooting and reduce the possibility that the soft young plants will develop fungal disease. Fertilize with a slow-release, high-nitrogen fertilizer four to six weeks after seed germination. Thereafter, adopt a regular fertilizing schedule (See page 70).

TIP: Generally, applying too much seed leads to a weak, overcrowded lawn. However, if you are planting into a living lawn, you should apply twice as much seed as recommended for bare ground, or plant according to the manufacturer's directions for overseeding.

TIP: Small-seeded grasses like bermudagrass and centipedegrass may be mixed thoroughly with fine soil or sand for spreading. Make sure the seed is distributed evenly in the added material. Account for the extra material when setting the spreading rate.

Test the spreading rate. Even though drop spreaders can be set to spread at a specified rate, they may not be as accurate as you'd like. To test the spread rate you've set, make a catcher out of a folded piece of cardboard and tie or tape it underneath the spreader hopper. Pour in some seed and roll the spreader forward as if you're covering a 100 sq. ft. area (for example, if your spreader lays a 2-ft.-wide band, go forward 50 ft.). Carefully remove the cardboard and weigh the seed it contains. Multiply the weight of the seed by ten to see how much the spreader would deposit over 1000 sq. ft at that setting. Adjust the chute opening accordingly.

Not sure if you've spread enough seed? Cut a square hole (3 × 3 in.) in a piece of paper. Position the paper with the hole over a representative patch of your newly-seeded yard. You should count from 70 to 100 seeds in the square. You will want slightly more seeds for bahiagrass and slightly fewer seeds for centipedegrass and buffalograss.

No-till Seeding

No-till planting can work for seeding and plugging lawns. You may chose not to till if the soil is not too hard and you haven't had to correct a serious pH problem, or add a lot of phosphorous, potassium or compost. Sloped land has more protection from erosion if you do not till. You may still add starter fertilizer, some compost and small amounts of non-hydrated lime or sulfur without tilling. Here are some recommended steps for preparing untilled ground for planting after killing the grass with solarization or herbicides:

1) Cut back the dead grass and vegetation with a lawn mower set at its lowest cutting height. Rake with a metal garden rake after mowing to scour the soil surface. This low mowing, called "scalping" is helpful if you will be seeding.

2) Add amendments like compost, starter fertilizer and, if called for by a soil test, lime or sulfur. Since you won't be tilling, you can't add more than 50 pounds of ground dolomite or calcitic limestone or 5 pounds of elemental sulfur per 1000 sq. ft. of lawn area. All amendments should be worked in with a power rake or aerator and then watered in thoroughly before planting seed. If you have thatch and you will be seeding, rip out the thatch with a power rake and remove it with a hand rake before spreading amendments.

3) Run over the lawn repeatedly with a power rake or verticutter and/or a core aerator. These will create loose, exposed dirt, which is desirable when you are planting seed. Seeds will also germinate in the holes left by a plug aerator. The plugs from a plug aerator can be broken up by dragging fencing or a rake over them. An untilled area is ready for seeding by standard methods when the soil surface is roughened and partly exposed. Now, follow seeding procedures as you would for any other lawn.

How to plant seed in untilled areas

1 Apply only low doses of fertilizers and amendments since you won't be tilling. You may split up a recommended dosage of burning materials like lime and sulfur and apply them over a number of years.

3 Seed a no-till lawn as you would any other. Notice that the ideal no-till seedbed has plenty of soft loose soil, which is essential for providing good seed-to-soil contact for maximum germination rates.

OPTION: Use a slit seeder. A slit seeder is a verticutter with a seed hopper. It can be used to deposit the seed in shallow furrows in the soil surface. This results in a more precisely, less wastefully planted lawn. As with other seeding methods, divide the seed you need to plant into two batches, then slit-seed the first batch in one direction and the second batch perpendicular to the first. Use a slit seeder on untilled ground instead of a power rake or non-seeding verticutter.

2 This power rake, set low, helps to work in amendments, and it provides loose soil for the seed to germinate in.

4 Rake lightly to bury about half the seed. Alternatively, top-dress with a thin layer of peat moss or compost. The seed should remain very close to the surface, and some seed should remain visible, even if you use the top-dress method.

5 Rolling with an empty or partially (no more than ¼) filled roller provides good seed-to-soil contact for germination.

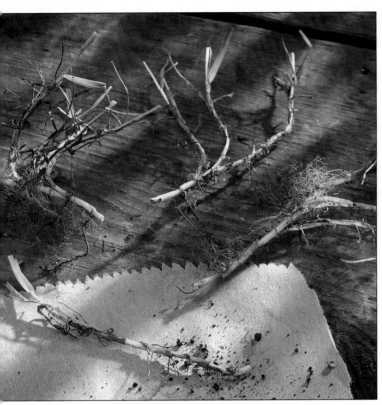

A "sprig" is a creeping-plant cutting that includes rhizomes or stolons, roots and leaves. You can cut them yourself from sod, or buy them by the bushel or bag from a nursery or mail-order catalog.

Whatever sprig-planting method you use (See next page), roll the soil after planting with a half-filled lawn roller to pack the sprigs in, improving their contact with the soil.

Planting a Lawn with Sprigs

Sprigs are often used to plant lawns in the South, since most of the warm-season grasses spread by root-like horizontal stems called rhizomes or by above-ground horizontal stems called stolons (See page 33). Sprigs are cuttings that include rhizomes and stolons, along with roots and leaves. Sprigs are heartier than seed, but aren't as bulky and expensive as sod. A large lawn can take truckloads of sod, but just bags of sprigs.

When to plant

For easiest lawn establishment, plant sprigs of warm-season grasses in late spring or early summer, just before warm-season grasses do their best growing. Wait until the soil has warmed to 65°F. Alternatively, plant sprigs during your summer rainy season, if you have one. A third option is to plant sprigs during the hot and dry parts of the summer, but this will require a lot of watering on your part.

Buying sprigs

You may buy sprigs by the bushel, or break up a yard or two of sod by hand or with a shredder to get a lot of sprigs. Generally, one square yard of sod will yield a bushel of sprigs. Each sprig should have two to four nodes from which roots can develop. Inferior sprigs are mostly greenish stolons without many roots, and they tend to be very leafy. These stolon sprigs dry out more easily than the rhizome sprigs, which are generally white with more roots, but still with leaves or green parts. Bermudagrass and zoysiagrass can produce good rhizome sprigs or poor stolon sprigs; look for ones made from shredded sod or otherwise dug out of the ground. Centipedegrass, St. Augustinegrass and buffalograss produce stolon sprigs only. It's better to plant these grasses from plugs (See page 66).

Know the square footage of your planting area before you go in search of sprigs. Broadcast planting methods consume much more sprig material than row planting: as much as 10 to 15 bushels per thousand square feet.

Usually, nurseries require you to order sprigs in advance, since they're a perishable product and they must order them from a supplier. When your sprigs arrive, keep them shaded and moist until planting.

Planting sprigs

To plant sprigs, take every bit as much care eliminating weeds and preparing the soil as you would for seed (see the checklist on page 48). For dry soil, water a couple of days before planting so the soil will be a little moist, but not wet. Make sure you are set up to water your newly-planted sprigs evenly and regularly after planting.

Weed Control: The preemergent herbicide simazine can be spread with some kinds of sprigs to prevent crabgrass and other grass weeds from sprouting from

PLANTING A LAWN FROM SPRIGS: 3 METHODS

Method 1: Grid planting. On soft soil, spread the sprigs 6 to 12 in. apart along straight lines that are 6 to 12 in. apart (closer plants fill in more quickly). Don't spread too many before setting them, since you don't want them exposed and baking in the sun. Push one end of each sprig into the soil with a notched stick or dull shovel. The end sticking out should have a leaf bud, leaf or node on it. Top-dress lightly with compost to protect the soil from drying. Roll the sprigs in with a half-filled lawn roller.

Method 2: Row planting. In harder soil, you can cut straight, 2-in.-deep furrows every 6 to 12 in., using a hoe. Angle the sprigs in the furrows 3 to 12 in. apart on center, leaving a part with green on it sticking up. Then, cover each sprig about two-thirds of the way with dirt while smoothing out the ridges and furrows. Cover lightly with compost and roll with a half-filled lawn roller.

seed (See page 50). Wait until after the second mowing or about a month after planting before spraying selective postemergent herbicides. The neat rows of the in-row planting methods make cultivating out weeds with a hoe possible, because you have straight, clear paths in between the sprigs.

Aftercare of a sprig lawn

After planting, mulching and spreading any pre-emergent herbicides, water deeply once, breaking the watering into ten-minute sessions if needed to avoid erosion, then follow the watering instructions on page 61 to keep the sprigs lightly and frequently watered until they sprout. Then, you can move gradually to deep, infrequent watering, which will help develop deep roots, control weeds and reduce disease potential. Top-dress with soil or compost occasionally to help the grass and to establish a more even lawn. Weed, cultivate or spray (after one month) regularly until the sprig lawn fully fills in. Fertilize lightly (1 pound nitrogen per 1000 sq. ft.) every six weeks with a slow-release, high-nitrogen fertilizer for the first growing season, then adopt a more moderate fertilizing schedule. Mow regularly to induce the grass to spread and to control weeds. Keep people and pets off the area until the grass fills in.

Method 3: Broadcasting. For the closest spacing and fastest-to-fill-in lawn, spread the sprigs randomly over the prepared ground and cover them with a thin layer of compost or a high-quality topsoil, then roll them in. Parts of the sprigs will poke up soon. Once this happens, spread a thin layer of straw mulch over them.

Plugs are small pieces of sod that are planted one at a time, then allowed to fill in over time.

Planting a Lawn with Plugs

Plugs are chunks of sod, 2 to 4 in. in diameter, that may be planted every 6 to 12 inches in small holes. Plugs may be purchased in trays or cut from sod and planted with a special tool. Plugs can save you a lot of money compared to sod, they will not dry out as fast as sprigs, they are easy to hoe between, and they often require the least soil preparation of any planting method. On the downside, they are labor intensive to plant. Start by going through the soil-prep checklist (page 48) to make sure you're ready for them. Water the soil a day or two before planting if it's dry, so the soil will be moist but not wet on the day of planting. Make sure you are set up to evenly and regularly water after planting. Know your lawn's square footage when buying plugs, so you can order the right quantity. You may plant them closer than recommended for a faster lawn, if you don't mind the extra work and expense.

Cut your own 2-in. plugs from sod with a plugging tool. Expect to use 10 to 15 square yards of sod per 1000 square feet for 6-in. spacing, and 3 to 5 square yards for 12-in. spacing.

Aftercare of a plug lawn

Keep pets and people off a newly-plugged lawn. Water deeply, then keep the plugs from drying out by watering once every day or two. Gradually, water less frequently and more deeply, encouraging the plugs to grow deep roots. Keep the spaces between the plugs hoed. Fertilize lightly (1 pound nitrogen per 1000 sq. ft.) every 6 weeks with a high-nitrogen fertilizer until the lawn fills in. Then, adopt a more moderate fertiliz-

Make a furrowing rake. Pound nails through a board at 6-in. intervals and drag this over your planting area. Make one set of parallel lines by over-scoring the far left line with the far right nail with every pass. Then, make lines perpendicular to the first set. This trick lets you make a checkerboard pretty quickly. Regular planting will make weed control a lot easier, since you'll be able to run down the rows and columns with a stirrup or scuffle hoe after the weeds sprout.

Plant at the intersections of the score lines, making sure the top of the plug is level with the soil. A bulb-hole digger, dibble, or a small trowel will come in handy. There's also a tool made for digging plug holes and chopping plugs from sod while standing up. After planting, consider mulching the plugs lightly with a fine compost. Straw will get in the way if you intend to hoe or cultivate weeds by hand. A plugged area should be rolled right after planting to avoid a tufted look.

ing schedule suitable for the species and your growing season. Mow regularly when rooted to control weeds and induce the grass to spread.

If soil between sprigs or plugs washes away, forming gullies, depressions, ridges or lumps, make sure to fill in the low spots with soil or compost so your finished lawn will be smooth.

Laying sod is probably the most common method for creating a new lawn, mostly because it offers instant results.

Laying Sod

Sod is a good choice for establishing a lawn on slopes and it will also suppress germinating weed seedlings and some perennial weeds. Most attractively, sod is green and lush from the start. On the negative, you may have little choice about what grasses you get when buying sod, and laying sod is the most expensive approach to establishing a lawn.

As with seed, sprigs and plugs, warm-season grass sod is best laid in the spring and cool-season sods in the early fall. But your flexibility is greater with sod than with planting. You can usually lay it anytime during the growing season, if you keep it watered every day for the first couple of weeks to one month. Check with local experts for suitable times to lay sod in your area.

Add up the total square footage of your yard to estimate the amount of sod you'll need, allowing 10 to 20% extra to compensate for wasted ends and edges. Find out how much the sod you're ordering weighs per square foot, then determine if you'll need to have it delivered or if you can haul it yourself. A full-size, one-ton pickup may carry 360 square feet (40 yards at most). Buy a few bags of compost or peat moss for filling in spaces left between pieces of sod (you can also use leftover topsoil). Use the sod the day you get it or roll it out in the shade and keep it watered.

Have pallets of sod delivered to your yard. If you can convince them to do it, have the delivery folks position the pallets so they're spaced apart evenly throughout the yard. This minimizes the need to move the sod, which is hard work and can cause damage.

Water, water, water. The key to getting sod to establish is to water it very heavily over the first month, soaking well through it every day and never allowing the roots and soil to dry out completely.

Preparing for sod

Although sod is fully-grown grass, its roots have been cut short. Sod needs almost as much attention as seed. Follow the same soil preparation directions that you would for any new lawn. Unlike seeding, however, you can't lay sod over existing grass without tilling. You will need to turn the soil or lay down new black dirt so that nothing comes between the roots of the sod and the soil. Water dry soil well a few days before laying sod so it is a little moist, but not sticky, on the day of sodding. Rake the soil before laying sod so it is loose and flat. Drag a ladder or large board with a rope tied at both ends over the dirt to create a more even base. Roll and rake again if your feet sink more than ½ in. into the soil when you step on it. Repeated rolling and raking is sometimes needed to achieve a smooth surface, but raking should always come last to leave the soil rough. Care should be taken to avoid over-compacting the soil.

Spot-check one roll per pallet of delivered sod to make sure both the top side and bottom side are healthy and free of insects and disease.

What to look for when you're buying sod

You can buy sod directly from a grower or from a nursery. Sod seldom is composed of a single species of grass. In the Upper Midwest, for example, typical "off-the-rack" sod is made up of a blend of four or five varieties of Kentucky bluegrass. You can judge the quality of sod with a simple, hands-on inspection. It should look healthy with rich green color and uniform density. It should have minimal thatch and there should be no signs of insect or disease on the top or bottom sides (check both). When a strip of healthy sod is grasped from opposite ends, it should not rip.

How to lay sod

1 Spread a 1- to 2-in.-thick layer of compost over the entire area, working the material in with a rototiller. This is not essential, but does provide an extra hedge against disease and drought for a newly sodded lawn.

2 Rake the soil level with a garden or landscape rake, removing lumps and debris in the process. Pull it in long passes to pick up even smallish particles.

3 Pull a lawn roller that's ⅓ full of water across the area to level out ridges and bumps. Fill any valleys or gaps with soil, then re-roll. Rake one last time to roughen the soil before laying sod.

How to lay sod

Lay the sod in a brick pattern, starting along the straight edge of a walk or drive or along a tight line in the middle of the yard. Stand on a board to avoid gouging up soft dirt or the newly laid sod. The long sides of the sod should run across slopes if possible, and be pinned in place if needed with stakes or metal staples.

The sod can be chopped with a sharp knife or a flat-edged garden spade. Join mismatched edges together by overlapping and chopping down through both pieces with a flat-edge spade and removing the ends. When finished, top-dress with fine topsoil, peat moss or compost to fill in the cracks, and roll the sod with a half-full roller to make good root-to-soil contact.

Aftercare of sod

Water the sod heavily right away, but avoid runoff or gullying under the sod by dividing this watering into a number of 10-minute sessions, if necessary. You want the soil wet to a depth of 6 in. Then, water lightly every day for a week or two to keep the soil under the sod moist until it establishes good, strong roots. Keep people and pets off the grass until it's well rooted. You will know when the sod is rooted because you won't be able to lift up pieces (although it's not recommended that you attempt this test too frequently). Gradually, you can move to less frequent watering to encourage the sod to root deeply.

Mow regularly once the grass is rooted. Set the mower blade high for the first season—for cool-season grasses, in particular. Long grass blades help the grass establish long, healthy roots. Fertilize four to six weeks after laying sod with a high-nitrogen, slow-release fertilizer. You may need additional topdressings of soil or compost if erosion, gaps or uneven settling is a problem.

TIP FOR SLOPES: Stake or staple sod in place on slopes. This will prevent gaps from opening along seams before the sod has a chance to root.

As an alternative to the "single-stack" method, sod may be laid parallel to adjacent sides of the lawn for more sod-side edging. Now the landscaper will lay subsequent rows parallel to the sidewalk, alternating the seams in a brick-like fashion.

4 Start at one corner of the planting area and lay sod around the perimeter first (Photo, left). Use full-width pieces on the outer edges so they don't dry out. Cut pieces to fit at seams with a utility knife. (Photo, above). Once the sod is down, roll it to remove air pockets, then water it immediately and deeply.

Yard Maintenance

Like any other kind of maintenance, taking care of a yard is mostly a matter of diligence. Performing routine, timely chores, like mowing and sprinkling, and seasonal procedures like dethatching and topdressing, is the surest way to keep your lawn healthy and avoid the need for "emergency" procedures.

Fertilizing

Of all routine lawn maintenance procedures, fertilizing requires the greatest precision. Over-fertilizing a lawn can burn the grass, kill beneficial soil organisms, promote thatch development, and even damage the structure of the soil. Under-fertilized turf grasses may appear thin and pale and have difficulty competing against broadleaf weeds better adapted to low-fertility conditions. It's a very good idea to get a soil test as the starting point of a successful fertilizing regimen (See page 49). A test will determine if you need to add high phosphorous or potassium fertilizers. The test will alert you to the need for any micronutrients, like iron, or the need to adjust the pH with lime or an acidifier. Tests let you know if you need to add organic matter too.

Nitrogen determines rate

Nitrogen is the queen of lawn maintenance fertilizers, and is the element that determines maintenance fertilizer application rates. That is, you calculate how much fertilizer to spread based on a yearly nitrogen budget for your lawn, letting the other elements be slightly over- or under-applied. You usually won't get a nitrogen analysis on a soil test, because nitrogen compounds can travel quickly out of the root zone in water. A high nitrogen reading could therefore be temporary. Instead, nitrogen appli-

A soil test can alert you to fundamental imbalances in your soil. Lime, sulfur, high phosphorous and potassium fertilizers and micronutrients can make big differences in the health of your lawn, but only if scientifically applied based on the recommendations of a soil lab. See page 49.

Fertilizer Calculation Table Based on Nitrogen Net Weight*	
4 pounds per 1000 square feet per year (Very high)	Apply if you regularly irrigate your bentgrass, bahiagrass, bermudagrass or St. Augustinegrass lawn, remove your clippings, and your grasses are actively growing for eight or more months of the year. Do not apply these high fertilizer rates to grasses with fungal diseases, insect problems or thatch buildup.
3 pounds per 1000 square feet per year (High)	Apply if conditions above apply, but you leave your clippings to rot. Apply if you irrigate and remove clippings on most bluegrasses, ryegrasses, tall fescue, carpetgrass and zoysiagrass. Apply a lower rate if thatch, disease or insect problems exist.
2 pounds per 1000 square feet per year (Medium)	Apply if you irrigate and remove clippings on low-maintenance grasses like the fine fescues, centipedegrass, blue gramagrass and buffalograss. High-maintenance grasses get two pounds if clippings are left to rot and they are not irrigated regularly.
1 pound per 1000 square feet per year (Low)	Apply to non-irrigated grasses when the clippings are left in place. Apply to low-maintenance grasses immediately if they are irrigated but the clippings are left in place. Apply to otherwise high-maintenance lawns that are dormant for much of the year due to winter cold, drought or summer heat.
0 pounds per 1000 square feet per year	Low-maintenance grasses may be left unfertilized or fertilized infrequently if clippings are returned to the soil and if the lawn is not irrigated. The existence (and acceptance) of clovers and medics in any lawn can reduce or eliminate the need for fertilizer, especially nitrogen. The regular addition of compost to a lawn can reduce or eliminate the need for fertilizer.

*Lawns in shade should receive ½ these rates to avoid disease problems. Adjust rates up on well-irrigated lawns and down on dry lawns.

cations are based on what kind of lawn you are after. Lawns fed more nitrogen will be greener but will need to be watered and mowed more. Lawns not fed at all may do fine, but they will have a higher percentage of non-grass plants in them.

NOTE: Plant-usable nitrogen enters soil naturally from three main sources: decaying plant and animal matter (including grass clippings) that return nitrogen and other elements to the soil; lightning in thunderstorms; and bacteria in the roots of pea and clover family plants that convert elemental nitrogen from the air into plant-usable forms.

Phosphorous, potassium & other elements

Phosphorous and potassium (sometimes called "potash") are less mobile in the soil than nitrogen and therefore may not need to be added at all. In the Deep South, some apply a complete fertilizer containing nitrogen, phosphorous and potassium in the spring and fall and just slow-release nitrogen in the summer. Get advice from local garden center experts or Extension Agents to see what's appropriate for your area. Soil tests give you phosphorous and potassium recom-

CORRECT pH

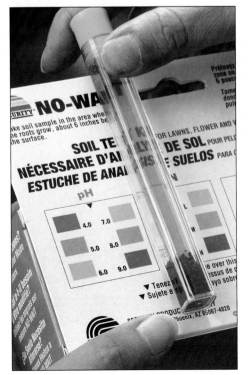

Correct pH (around seven or a little below) is needed so that grass can access nutrients already in the soil. If you have acid (low pH) or alkaline (high pH) soil, a soil test will determine how much limestone to add to raise the pH or how much of an acidifier (such as sulfur) to add to bring down the pH. pH meters and simple testing kits are also available from garden centers.

mendations specific to your yard, letting you know if you should be using a maintenance fertilizer high in one or both of these elements. A soil test may also recommend the addition of one of the secondary elements, or "micronutrients." Adding micronutrients without the recommendation of a soil test is risky, since many are toxic to plants at relatively low concentrations. However, in some parts of the country adding micronutrients like iron can be essential for achieving a healthy lawn. For soils with special problems, special soil conditioners are recommended by soil labs. For example, on high-salt soils of the West, gypsum is often added.

Buying fertilizer & other amendments; calculating quantities

By convention, fertilizer bags always give the weight percentages of nitrogen (N), phosphorous (P) and potassium (K), in that order. This allows you to adjust the application rate of a particular fertilizer to a recommended rate of application. For example, say you want to apply two pounds of nitrogen per thousand square feet per year in two applications. That means at each application you will spread one pound of nitrogen per 1000 square feet. Say that, because of a soil test, you know you don't need any phosphorous. You should buy a 50-pound bag of fertilizer with an analysis of 10:5:0. Fifty pounds times 10% (.10) nitrogen equals five pounds of nitrogen.

Let's say that earlier, you determined that your lawn was about 1,500 sq. ft. 1,500 sq. ft. times the recommended rate of 1 pound/1000 sq ft. (per application) equals 1.5 pounds of nitrogen. 1.5 divided by five pounds (the total nitrogen in the bag), gives you 0.3, meaning you need to spread three-tenths, or a little less than one-third, of the bag onto your lawn. If you like formulas, we've provided the one used here below. Incidentally, compost usually has a fertilizer value around 1-1-1.

Buy a fertilizer with at least half its nitrogen in slow release form. Slow-release nitrogen includes IBDU, sulfur-coated urea, urea-formaldehyde (Nitroform, for example) and natural organics such as Milorganite or composted cow manure. Slow-release and natural products last longer, are less likely to burn your grass, and will leach less nitrate into surface waters or the groundwater.

FERTILIZER RATE TO AMOUNT OF BAG FORMULA:

Pounds Recommended/1000 sq. ft. × size of lawn in sq. ft. = pounds of nitrogen (N) needed.

Pounds N in bag = Percentage N/100 × net weight of bag.

Pounds N needed/Pounds N in bag = numbers of bags (or fraction of bag) needed.

READING FERTILIZER BAGS

The fertilizer in this bag is 18% nitrogen, 22% phosphorous and 6% potassium by weight. Since a pound of the fertilizer contains .18 pounds of nitrogen, you would need about five-and-a-half pounds of the fertilizer to give you one pound of nitrogen. The whole 18-pound bag contains about 3¼ pounds of nitrogen.

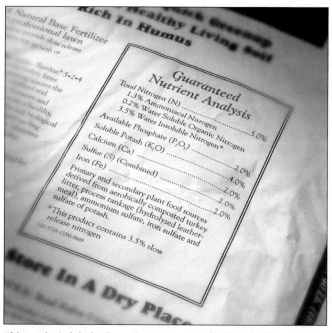

This analysis label tells us that nitrogen is 5% of the fertilizer by weight. Importantly, it also tells us that 3.5% of the fertilizer, or more than two-thirds of the nitrogen, is slow-release nitrogen.

How often, how much & when to fertilize

Quick-release fertilizers should be applied at a rate of no more than 1 pound of nitrogen per 1000 sq. ft. at one time, and slow-release fertilizers should be applied no heavier than 2 pounds of nitrogen per 1000 sq. ft. at a time. If you employ multiple fertilizer applications in one year, it is best to decide ahead of time the total quantity of nitrogen you will spread in the year. This will enable you to determine how much nitrogen should be applied at each application. Naturally, with multiple applications you may be applying fertilizer rates in a single application that are below those recommended on the bag.

Apply fertilizer in the afternoon when the grass is completely dry. The best time of year to fertilize warm-season grasses is during their growing season in the late spring and summer. Use only slow-release fertilizer on warm-season lawns in the summer to prevent burn. In the Coastal Deep South

TOPDRESSING

Topdressing makes a little fertilizer go a long way. Chemical fertilizers and some pesticides can reduce microorganism populations, making elements in the soil unavailable for plant uptake. Topdressing with compost, composted manure or rich topsoil provides nitrogen, phosphorous and potassium (NPK) and carbon compounds. The carbon compounds feed the soil microorganisms. Soil organisms not only make NPK available to plants, they keep disease organisms in check. If you top-dress yearly, you may reduce or eliminate fertilizer applications. Apply ½ to 1 cubic yard of well-composted material or topsoil per 1000 sq. ft. of lawn with a rake or peat spreader.

(Zone E on our Grass Climate Map, page 34), you may fertilize in the spring and fall before considering a summer application, since fall fertilization can help warm-season grasses build up reserves for winter. Fall fertilization of warm-season grasses is dangerous too far north, since frost damage of over-stimulated grasses can occur. Ideally, a fall fertilizer application should be low in phosphorous and relatively high in nitrogen and potassium.

The best time to fertilize cool-season grasses is when they are actively growing in the fall. High-maintenance grasses may receive a late spring application, but avoid early spring applications. Also, never apply fertilizer close to or during summer dormancy. The grass should not be encouraged to

grow lush top growth just before the heat of the summer, and nitrogen that does not get used by grass will only help fertilize summer weeds.

Important: Only fertilize dry grass. Fertilizer will stick to damp grass and burn the blades.

Watch your pH balance

You may need to adjust the pH over the period of a year with two or three lime or acidifier applications. Apply no more than 50 pounds of ground dolomite or calcitic limestone or 5 pounds of elemental sulfur per 1000 sq. ft. of established lawn at one time.

Applying Fertilizers & Other Amendments

Fertilizers, limestone, gypsum and other substances must be spread as evenly as possible to achieve optimal results and to avoid damaging the lawn. You probably don't need a scale, but do take the time to pour the fertilizer you will use into a clean bucket or another bag. Be sure to write on the bag how much unused fertilizer is left. By dividing a bag of fertilizer with a known net weight ahead of time, your application weights will be more precise.

Once you've got the quantity you want to spread, divide it into two approximately equal portions. Load one of the portions into your drop or broadcast spreader. If your spreader is calibrated for the brand of fertilizer you're using, that's great. Set the spreader to disperse the fertilizer at half the rate you'll be applying. Otherwise, aim low. It's better to spread too thin and have to take another pass than to spread too heavily. Disperse your first load in one of the patterns shown in the illustrations to the left, as it's easier to cover the edges first. This way you can spread up to, but not beyond, the borders of the lawn. When you fill in the middle, you'll want to release the spread lever or button before U-turning over the edges you've already fertilized.

Now, load in the other half of the fertilizer. Adjust the calibration as needed, and begin spreading in a pattern perpendicular to the first. You may need to do the edges as you did them the first time, but the crisscross pattern in the middle will help even out the application and prevent striping. When you're done, wash out your spreader well, particularly if it's made of metal, since fertilizer is corrosive.

Use the two-batch method to spread fertilizer. Divide the total volume of fertilizer you'll be applying into two equal parts. Adjust your spreader to provide coverage that's half of the recommended coverage rate. Fill the spreader with half of the fertilizer and spread it evenly onto the entire area. Add the other half and spread it over the first pass, operating the spreader at perpendicular angles to the first run. This helps ensure very even fertilizer coverage.

SPREADING PATTERNS

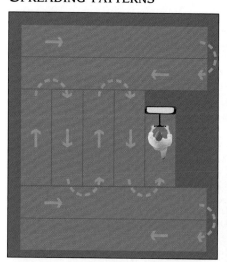
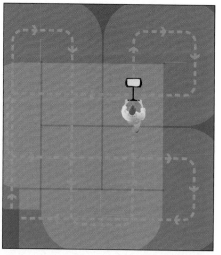

Use one of the patterns shown above as a model for spreading fertilizer with a drop spreader. The best approach is to start at the edges of the area being fertilized, then fill in the middle area. When using the two-batch method described above, you may need to retrace your steps at the edges when you make the second pass, but work at perpendicular angles to the original pattern whenever possible.

When to Fertilize Your Lawn

Cool-season grasses (northern climate)

Annual rate of nitrogen

Spread one pound at a time (complete fertilizer)	Divide evenly for application on these dates
4 pounds N/1000 ft²	4 applications: August, September, October-November, May-June
3 pounds N/1000 ft²	3 applications: August, October-November, May-June
2 pounds N/1000 ft²	2 applications: August, October-November
1 pound N/1000 ft²	1 application: September

This fertilizer timing chart for Minnesota illustrates that cool-season grasses prefer to be fed before periods of cool, wet weather.

Warm season grasses (southern climate)

Note: summer applications are not recommended when disease or insects are a problem.

Annual rate of nitrogen

Spread one pound of total N at a time. Use a complete fertilizer (NPK) in the spring; Slow-release N only in the heat of late spring and summer; and a complete fertilizer low in P in the late summer or fall (where fall fertilizer is appropriate).	Total nitrogen divided evenly for application at these dates
4 pounds N/1000 ft² (common bermudagrass, Gulf Coast)	April 1, May 1, June 1, August 1
3 pounds N/1000 ft² (common bermudagrass, Central Miss.)	May 1, June 1, August 1
2 pounds N/1000 ft² (centipedegrass, Gulf)	April 1, August 1
1 pound N/1000 ft² (centipedegrass, Central Miss.)	May 1

This fertilizer timing chart for Mississippi illustrates that warm-season grasses prefer to receive most of their fertilizer prior to the hot months. It also cautions that phosphorous, potassium, and quick-release nitrogen can harm grass if applied in hot weather.

Cool-season Grasses

Soluble nitrogen produces a burst of top-growth in grass plants. Rampant growth can work against the long-term health of the lawn, particularly if it comes at the wrong time. A common (but ill-advised) practice is to apply fertilizer to cool-season grasses at the first signs of greening in the spring. This over-stimulates growth, which depletes carbohydrate reserves in the roots. The overgrown blades are soft and susceptible to disease, late frost and insects. As the weakened grasses come under attack, the same fertilizer used to plush-up the grass is raising a healthy crop of annual weeds that are well adapted to use the excess nitrogen. Disappointed homeowners finally put on herbicides and more fertilizer come summer. Now it has become too hot for the cool-season grasses to benefit from the nitrogen. Instead, warm-season weed grasses like crabgrass take the fertilizer and run.

The correct way to fertilize cool-season grasses is with an early fall application of a balanced, slow-release fertilizer. This allows the grass to soak up solar energy and stock their roots with carbohydrates and other fertilizer elements before winter. Come spring, the grass is ready for sustained, even grown, and nothing is left for the weeds.

Warm-season Grasses

Fertilizing warm-season grasses too much and too early can cause the same problems described above for their northern cousins, especially if quick-release nitrogen is used. The tops of the grass grow too lushly and too fast while the roots languish in cool soil, inviting disease, insect and late-frost destruction of leaves. Since the roots are low on carbohydrate reserves, they cannot push up replacement leaves indefinitely. Instead, a well-fertilized crop of weeds takes over. That's why southern Extension Agents usually recommend waiting three or four weeks into the growing season before fertilizing warm-season grasses. Since the warm-season grasses like heat, you might apply fertilizer during the summer on a high-maintenance lawn. Summer fertilization becomes unnecessary or harmful if the grass goes dormant or if a summer disease or insect problem exists. There is nothing pests and disease like more than soft, overfed grass. The application of a late-summer or early-fall fertilizer that's low in phosphorous and high in potassium and slow-release nitrogen (e.g. a 2-1-2 ratio) can promote root development and carbohydrate storage during a long, mild fall growing season. This puts the grass in good position to come back strong in the spring. Do not fertilize too close to winter weather, since nitrogen inhibits dormancy. Ask a local expert when the last safe date to apply fertilizer in your area is.

Watering

As a rule, lawns stay healthiest with infrequent but deep watering. Frequent shallow watering promotes thatch buildup, annual-weed growth and disease, and "spoils" the lawn by concentrating all the feeder roots in the top inch of soil. Deep watering builds resilient, deep-rooted lawns that survive cold, heat, drought and insects better. Here are some tips for watering your lawn effectively:

Don't water by hand. A deep watering can take an hour or more. Select a sprinkler or sprinklers that can be set up to deliver an even spray to all parts of your lawn. For time efficiency, position multiple sprinklers around an area, and use Y-connectors and extra hoses to run them simultaneously. Try to use the same kind of sprinkler everywhere for consistent coverage, and avoid inconsistent overlaps of sprinkler patterns.

The ideal sprinkler has a distribution pattern that matches or can be matched to the shape you are trying to water. The flow rate should not exceed the ability of your lawn to absorb the water, and the sprinkler should deliver water uniformly, without creating overly wet areas near the base of the sprinkler.

Soak the soil six to eight inches down. Typically, this will take about an inch of water, although very sandy soils may take half that and a heavy clay can take twice that. For heavy clay soils, you may need to apply water in short 10-minute sessions, spaced 10 minutes apart to avoid runoff. This is only practical with a programmable water timer. If you have thatch or compaction problems in your yard, your lawn may absorb less than 5 minutes of water at a time from a high-flow sprinkler or irrigation system. Adjust your watering schedule accordingly, but deal with the thatch as soon as possible.

GAUGING WATER AMOUNTS

To gauge how much water you've applied to your lawn, arrange tuna-fish cans or other straight-sided cans at incremental distances from the sprinkler and monitor the depth of the water as the sprinkler runs. Better sprinklers will fill all the cans evenly, but you'll probably need to average between the cans. Overlapping multiple sprinklers will provide more even coverage.

Let the lawn completely dry before watering again. Constant damp conditions encourage weed, disease and insect problems. Probe the soil with a screwdriver or use an earth auger or a moisture meter to see if the soil has dried to a 6 to 8-in. depth. Drying could take two or three weeks for a heavy clay soil or a matter of days for a sandy soil.

Important: New lawns and sod should be watered more frequently and for shorter times until the roots are well established. A new lawn in hot weather may need to be watered briefly three or four times a day.

Water conservation

Deep-rooted grasses like tall fescue, bermudagrass, zoysiagrass and buffalograss can be watered so that the ground is moist 12 in. down 24 hours after watering, and then not watered again until the soil dries to that depth. This will train your grass to root deeply, taking better advantage of deep rainfalls and stored water.

In dry areas, your water utility service, the Cooperative Extension Agency, or even the newspaper can provide average evapotranspiration (ET) figures for grass in your area for any particular month. If your rate is ".2," that means your grass (in full sun) must receive .2 in. of rain or irrigation water per day (1.4 in. per week). Notice that the frequency of watering will still depend on how many inches of water your lawn can absorb at one time. Be aware that lawn ET rates are 20 to 40% less than the generic, base ET rates that are averaged out for all plants. If your newspaper's ET is not specifically for grass, contact your Cooperative Extension Service to determine the conversion factor.

The Freedom Lawn

Assuming it's acceptable in your neighborhood, any lawn can be treated as a "freedom lawn," a term coined by the authors of the classic book *Redesigning the American Lawn*. Rather than water a freedom lawn, one lets it adapt to dry conditions by going brown and dormant. This works in most parts of the country for the most prevalent grass species; however, some species of grass, such as Kentucky bluegrass and St. Augustinegrass, may actually die under prolonged drought conditions. Even drought-tolerant grasses like zoysiagrass and bermudagrass can die if a drought is long enough. Your local Cooperative Extension Service can recommend grass and groundcover mixes adapted to a low-maintenance regimen for your climate and soil conditions.

TESTING FOR MOISTURE

Moisture meters provide an easy, non-destructive way to test soil moisture at varying depths. They can be found at any garden center.

CHECKING DEPTH OF WATER PENETRATION

Probe your soil with a spade, trowel or an earth auger (with a cut-away window) before, then 12 hours after watering to see how far the water has penetrated. Waiting 12 or even 24 hours before probing clay soil is needed because water moves very slowly through clay soil. This is a reliable method, but obviously is more disruptive to the lawn than a moisture meter (top of page).

HOSE ACCESSORIES

A Y-connector with dual shutoff valves allows you to turn one hose bib into two, each with a shutoff. Brass Y-connectors are more durable than plastic Y-connectors, which can spring leaks under high pressure.

Quick connectors are two-part assemblies that allow you to change sprinklers in a hurry. One connector part is screwed onto the end of a hose or a hosebib; the other end is screwed onto the port on a sprinkler or hose. The two parts snap together in the same fashion as air compressor hose connectors, and create a reliably leak-free connection.

SPRINKLING TIMERS

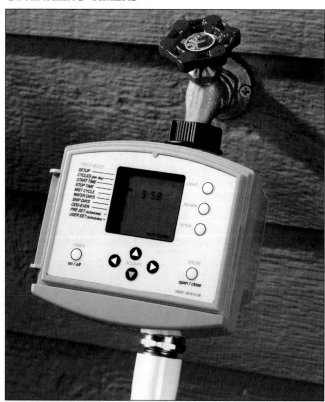

Sillcock timers. The better water timers attach directly to your sillcock, so the hose isn't left under pressure when the automatic valve shuts. Programmable electronic timers can be set to water in repeating cycles, which is useful if your soil absorbs water slowly.

On-board sprinkler timers. The oscillating sprinkler above has an integral water timer. Such a timer requires a sturdy, leak-free hose, and even then, you may not want to leave it unattended. But they are a cost-effective option to sillcock timers (left).

Repairing a garden hose

Pierced hose or leaking connector? Don't throw away an otherwise perfectly good garden hose: Repair it instead.

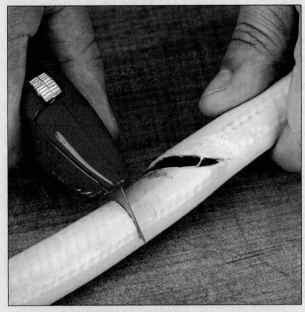

1 Cut out the damaged section of hose with a utility knife. Measure the inside diameter of your hose so you can purchase a repair coupling of the correct size. Hardware stores carry a variety of easy-to-use repair products for damaged hoses, including male and female ends and hose-to-hose connectors. Most employ a barbed coupling (brass are better than nylon) that slips into each cut end of the hose to make the repair joint.

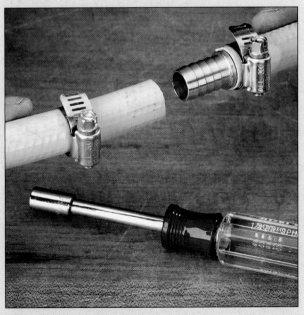

2 Loosely slip a hose clamp onto each mating end of the cut hose, then insert an end of the barbed coupling into each hose section. Position the hose clamps over the coupling in each section and tighten the clamps.

A rolling cart/hose reel simplifies garden hose management.

Hoses, carts & reels

If you ever need to deliver a constant flow of water more than 50 ft. away from your primary sillcock, you have a decision to make when it comes to garden hose. Decent quality garden hoses are sold in lengths of 50, 75 and 100 ft. You'll want to consider purchasing the 75 or 100-foot hose for maximum reach without joining multiple hoses together (and creating the inevitable leaks at the connections). If you go with the longer hose, consider a hose reel or hose cart to keep it organized. But if the bulk of the watering you do is within the 50-ft. range, or reachable with a sprinkler from a point 50 ft. away from the sillcock, consider the shorter hose. You may need to attach an extension hose to it occasionally, but you'll avoid the constant battle that comes with trying to manage all that extra hose. In either case, ⅝-in.-dia. hose is a better choice than ½-in., because it's less likely to restrict water flow. Five-ply is better than 4-ply when purchasing rubber/vinyl combination hoses. All-rubber hoses tend to be high quality, but they're more expensive and a bit heavy to lug around. Better quality garden hoses have brass fittings, not plastic or vinyl.

A. Spinning Style

D. Oscillating Style

B. Adjustable Style

C. Sprinkler Hose

E. Impulse Style

F. Soaker Hose

G. Self-propelled

Sprinklers

Spinning sprinklers **(A)** have uneven distribution and low throw radius, making these a generally poor choice. Inexpensive adjustable sprinklers **(B)** that offer a choice of spray patterns can work for small areas if you don't water much, and they can work with low water pressure. But these are not a good solution for regular waterers, since they often leak and have uneven distribution patterns. Sprinkler hoses **(C)** work well for long, awkward shapes and on slopes, since their low flow rate does not exceed the ability of the soil to absorb water. They are difficult to set up for even coverage. The better quality oscillating sprinklers **(D)** allow you to adjust the width and sweep of the rectangular-shaped spray pattern, and the gentle spray is good for newly seeded areas and clay soils that absorb water slowly. However, they lose more water to evaporation than other sprinklers. Quality metal impulse sprinklers **(E)** are durable and lay down a lot of water in a large circular or semi-circular pattern. Distribution is uniform. Their high flow rate can cause runoff on high-clay soils if watering isn't broken up into short sessions. Soaker hose **(F)** is normally installed semi-permanently in planting beds under a layer of mulch. Self-propelled sprinklers **(G)** use water pressure to move slowly along a track formed by your hose. These can be perfect for oblong alleys of lawn (plus, they're kind of fun to watch). Don't make them take sharp corners or travel over rough terrain.

In-ground sprinkler systems

In-ground sprinkler systems are gaining popularity as a labor-saving tool that rigorously maintains a watering schedule. Even if you have no intention of installing a system yourself (it's really not that hard to do), if you have an in-ground system you'd be well advised to understand its basic components and how they work.

Well-attended in-ground sprinkler systems can maintain an even, green lawn with as little water (and labor) as possible. They can be programmed for zone watering, so areas that require less water, such as perennial planting beds, are watered less frequently than thirstier areas. Because they water your yard automatically, you can head to the spa for a few days of recovery after laying sod, and be confident that the new sod will get the water it needs in your absence. They can even improve the resale value of your house—especially if you have a very large yard. There are plenty of good reasons these up-and-coming mechanical systems are gathering a lot of interest.

Traditionally, installing and maintaining in-ground sprinkler systems has been left to contractors. But in case you're feeling ambitious (and a little thrifty), you can also purchase the components and install a system yourself. System distributors even offer free system design services.

Measuring your water flow rate

Before you can choose and design an in-ground sprinkler system, you'll need to determine the rate and pressure at which water flows through your plumbing. If you can't locate a gauge like the one shown to the right, test this way:

• Attach an ordinary water pressure gauge to a faucet inside your house and open the faucet all the way.

• Turn on your exterior sillcock full blast. Check the pressure on the gauge inside the house. If it's less than 35 PSI, turn down the sillcock until the pressure climbs up to 35 PSI.

• Without changing the rate of flow from the sillcock, time how long (in seconds) it

Available water flow and pressure will impact how many heads, and of what type, you can install in each "valve zone." You can measure both water pressure and flow with a gauge like the one shown above—you may be able to borrow one from your irrigation system distributor.

takes to fill a 5-gallon bucket. Divide 300 by the number of seconds to calculate your rate of flow in gallons per minute (GPM).

Sprinkler Heads

The type of sprinkler head you choose should be determined by the size and nature of the watering zones in your yard, as well as your budget.

Pop-up height. Lawn sprinkler heads pop up out of the ground under water pressure. Even in landscaping borders, these are preferable to shrub-style heads, which stay up all the time. Pop-up models come in different heights. Professionals usually install heads that pop up 4 in. Anything less than a 3-in. pop-up is not recommended. Heads for garden or shrub borders should pop up higher: as much as 12 in.

Material. Brass sprinkler heads will last longer than plastic, and they may provide a more even flow, but the good ones cost much more than good plastic heads, which are more than adequate for just about any residential installation. Plastic or brass, look for heads with a spring for retracting the nozzle (some rely on gravity), and a separate, well-fitting wiper seal to keep water from running out between the riser and housing.

A typical plastic, pop-up sprinkler.

Rotor or fixed? Last, you need to choose between a rotor-style head and a fixed head. The rotor style sends rotating streams of water out from the head in about a 30-ft. radius. They cover more ground per head, but they are more expensive, and they require at least 40 pounds per square inch (PSI) of water pressure. Fixed heads usually spray a 15-ft. radius. If you have a small lot, you're better off going with the fixed head. These are easier to adjust and maintain. Whatever kind of heads you get, they will demand a minimum amount of water flow, which will figure into how you set up the system: specifically, whether you can feed the system from the sillcock, or will need to tie directly into your water supply system to get sufficient water pressure.

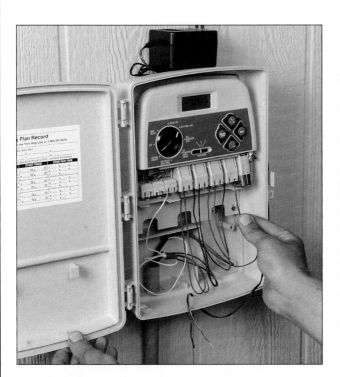

The Timer

The timer is a programmable control panel that is wired directly to the valves controlling the flow of water into the irrigation system. Through electronic impulses it opens and closes the valves according to the multi-zone watering schedule you plug in.

Tubing & Fittings

The sprinkler heads are connected to the supply valves with a network of flexible poly tubing and PVC pipe fittings. Most of the joints between tubing and fittings are secured with pipe clamps.

The Valve Manifold

The valve manifold is the cluster of automatic or manual valves that distribute water to each of the individual watering zones. It is usually located in an underground box next to the foundation of the house. The manifold is connected directly to the main water supply for the house (the supply line to the system needs to be fitted with a backflow prevention device). Each valve in the manifold controls one specific zone, called a "valve zone." Supply tubing runs from the valve in a branch supply line. At each sprinkler head, tubing that supplies the head is connected to the branch originating at the valve.

When running supply "branch lines" from the manifold, try to come up with an efficient path that minimizes trenching—sharing a trench with another branch line is a good way to obtain this goal.

It's a good idea to put filters downstream of the valves. These can save you the headache of replacing clogged sprinkler nozzles, since the high flow of irrigation systems tend to carry sand and other particles from the water supply into the system.

Note to Northerners: Even if your valve manifold is at a high point among the branch lines to the sprinkler heads, you may still need a drain valve in the manifold that is accessible through the valve box opening—it depends on the type and manufacturer of your irrigation system. The drain valve is opened to drain the system before winter, and is often attached to a drain pipe.

The Valve Box

The valve box contains and protects the valve manifold. It is usually heavy plastic with a removable, bolt-on cover that's kept level with the ground. The box should rest on a bed of gravel.

Backflow prevention device

Drip line

Main water supply

Branch supply lines

Valve manifolds

Branch supply lines

Valve box (covered)

Valve box (uncovered)

Miscellaneous fittings include: *Replacement flow nozzles (left)* inserted to change the pattern of an in-ground sprinkler head; *Saddle fitting (middle)* used to locate sprinklers directly over supply lines or to provide a tap for flexible tubing extensions; *Flexible extension tubing (right)* used to locate sprinklers off of main lines without having to extend main supply lines off of their direct path.

SYSTEM VARIATION: Automatic Drip Lines

Drip lines utilize an additional pressure reducer after the valve.

Drip lines are staked in planting beds and covered with mulch.

In-ground watering systems can be equipped with drip lines instead of sprinkler heads. Drip lines provide a slow, constant supply of water to confined areas, like small planting beds, or around specimen trees. They are run as dedicated lines from the valve manifold, not tacked onto sprinkler lines.

Designing your in-ground sprinkler system

To build a successful irrigation system, you need to know exactly what you are irrigating. Draw the area to be irrigated to scale on graph paper. It's best to put parts of buildings in first and develop the rest of the map by measuring off them. When the broad outlines of fences, garden beds, buildings and pavement are noted, sketch in objects like trees, bushes, grills and play areas.

Map the sprinkler circuits

Before you can proceed with any drawings of the sprinkler system layout, you'll have to decide which type of sprinkler heads you want your system to have—this is actually kind of a back-and-forth process of trying to reconcile the shapes and ranges of the sprinkler heads that are available with the shapes and sizes of the areas in your yard. You'll want to have a complete catalog of options from the manufacturer during this process. Here are some tips:

• You want as many of the heads as possible to be up against the borders and corners of the lawn, where they are out of harm's way.

• At borders, you'll want heads that spray in 180° patterns. At corners, a 90° pattern is preferred.

• Once you've established the perimeter, fill in the middle, staggering the heads in a triangle pattern for greatest efficiency.

• Sprinklers should spray head-to-head, which means each head is separated from its neighbors by the radius of its spray. More widely spaced heads will produce an uneven watering pattern. Manufacturers provide different ways of reducing the spraying radius of individual heads when necessary, and most also provide a head for long, narrow spaces.

Watering zones

One of the benefits of zone irrigation is the ability to provide different levels of water to different

Draw a scale map of your yard, including planting beds, that notes any special watering requirements. Then, after choosing a sprinkler head type and determining how many sprinkler heads can be supported by each system of heads, plot out possible watering patterns that effectively divide your yard into watering zones.

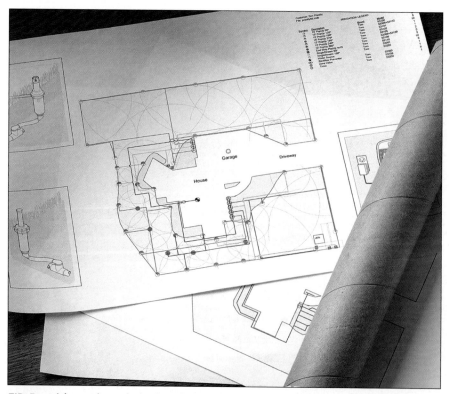

TIP: For tricky yards, work closely with the in-ground system dealer or manufacturer. Some suppliers will generate sprinkler head patterns for you on a computer if you provide them with a scaled map of your yard.

parts of the yard, depending on how much water each area needs. You could create a low-water hydro-zone for your shrubs, for example, a medium-water zone for your perennials, and a high-water zone for your lawn. Shady parts of the lawn can receive less water, as long as a thirsty tree isn't responsible for the shade. You could even set up a zone of drip emitters to conserve on water. Factor these watering zones into your master plan drawing.

Valve zones

A valve zone includes all the sprinkler heads that lead back to a particular control valve. You can have more than one valve zone in a watering zone, but you can't have a single valve zone cross between two watering zones. The size of the valve zone is determined by the number of gallons per minute (GPM) your water supply system can provide, as well as the operating water pressure available to the irrigation system (See page 82): these system capacities will dictate how many heads can be installed per valve zone, since all the heads in a valve zone go on at the same time. Usually, the GPM demand load within a valve zone should be no more than 75% of the GPM flow your supply system can provide. Valves, pipe and elevation impact the actual GPM available at the sprinkler heads. Use the sprinkler head manufacturer's charts to figuring out how many heads can go in one valve zone. It's safer to err on the side of caution and stay safely below the GPM rate that's (theoretically) available.

Maintaining an Underground Sprinkler System

Test the laterals and heads

Hit the bleeder valve or turn on your manual knob to see a valve's sprinkler heads. Most likely they'll come telescoping out of the ground and start rotating, or they will spray water in a fixed pattern. Notice that the heads are arranged to provide complete coverage within the station. Does it look like all the heads came up? Are the heads distributing water evenly? Is water spraying on a surface it shouldn't? If you leave the water on for a while, do you get a muddy spot or water coming out of the ground anywhere? Mark problem areas before turning off the station and moving on to the next.

Unclogging or replacing a sprinkler-head nozzle or drip emitter

Sometimes you need only to unclog the nozzle or reposition the spray head to get it to work right. Clogged sprinkler nozzles can be flushed or replaced. Drip emitter heads can also be removed and cleaned if they become clogged. While nozzles and emitter heads are off, flush out the system's pipes by running the water. You may need to protect the sprinkler heads with pieces of hose, so dirty water doesn't get sucked into the openings when you turn their valves off.

Replacing heads or risers

Leaks near or at a head that won't pop up may require that you replace the sprinkler head or the riser. The riser is the length of tubing that connects the head to the lateral line.

Fixing a broken pipe

Broken or leaking pipes show up as muddy spots or bubbling springs that appear when the station is on. Dig down to the problem area using the bleeder valve to reveal the leak if necessary. Dig around and below the damage so you have plenty of room to work without getting dirt in the line. With PVC, you may cut out the damaged area squarely with a hack saw and purchase a piece of pipe of the same size, two repair couplers, sandpaper, PVC solvent cement and primer (for one repair, you may get by with just the cement, but the primer will form a more solid weld). Sand the rough-cut pipe ends, apply the primer and cement as directed on the labels, and stick everything together. You'll need to wait a day for the solvent weld to cure before you can turn the water back on to test your fix. If you have black polyethylene supply tubing (PE), you'll cut the pipe at the leak and make the repair with a brass coupling that inserts into the pipe ends and is held on to the pipe with hose clamps.

Resetting the control box using 'soil based' watering

The control box will be found in a garage, basement, or utility room. It houses the timers for putting water on the different zones. Figure out the timing by manually operating the zones first, monitoring soil moisture levels before and the day after watering. Most lawn grasses should be watered when the soil dries below 6 in. More drought-adapted plants tolerate or even prefer periods of dry soil between rain or irrigation. When you do water, though, it should be deeply.

Your lawn or garden soil may be unable to absorb all the water it needs at one time without runoff and puddling. With your control box, you can set the system to cycle through the zones repeatedly, allowing each area to receive its full "dose" of water in a series of short waterings. This gives the water time to sink in. If you need to apply less than five minutes of water at a time, your lawn is probably ready for dethatching or aeration.

HOW THE PRO'S DO IT: Installing an in-ground sprinkler system

The following sequence provides a glimpse into the installation process for a complete in-ground sprinkler system. Even among professionals installation techniques vary, and in this project, as with any project, adjustments and adaptations were made owing to unique circumstances the installers encountered. Because the system was installed in a northern climate, the placement of water supply pipes and the installation of a backflow prevention device were done according to codes for cold weather. In warmer climates, the codes and procedures will differ.

Special thanks to The Toro Co. and Anderson Irrigation Systems of Elk River, Minnesota.

Before | After

1 Update plumbing, if needed. This home's plumbing, between the water meter and the hot water heater, needed to be updated to accommodate the increased flow requirements of a sprinkler system. The existing ¾-in.-dia. supply pipe was replaced with 1-in.-dia. pipe. In addition, the new supply is split into two lines, each with its own shutoff valve. One line goes to the water heater to supply the home's indoor needs and the other goes out through the side of the house to supply the sprinkler system.

2 The project began with a groundbreaking. First, utility lines that had been flagged were carefully exposed with a shovel so there would be no awful surprises once the power digging got underway.

3 The power trencher cuts through the soil and pulls the tubing down into the trench in one operation. This results in a much faster and cleaner installation process. Many irrigation contractors will subcontract this part of the job for you or you can rent a power trencher and do it yourself. Or, you can always dig the trenches the old-fashioned way, with a trenching shovel.

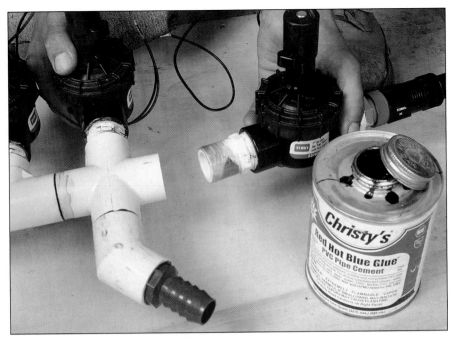

4 As the trenching and laying of tubing was going on outside, another crew member got busy assembling the valve manifold. The control valves are solvent-welded to PVC pipe to make the assembly.

Vacuum breaker

Cleanout plug

5 Codes require that a backflow prevention device is installed in the supply line at a point higher than the highest sprinkler head (this prevents water from backing up into the clean water supply system). The supply pipe for the irrigation system was fed through the foundation wall and connected to the updated supply plumbing near the water main. Then a vacuum breaker on a U-bend was attached, along with a cleanout plug for system maintenance and draining.

6 The main supply from the house is connected to the poly tubing for the system with double hose clamps. The joint is about 12 in. underground.

7 (RIGHT) The programmable timer that's the brains of the system was mounted on the garage wall (in some areas it must be inside) and the process of wiring the controls for each individual zone was begun. Each pair of wires controls a separate valve in the valve manifold, where the connections at the other end of the run are made.

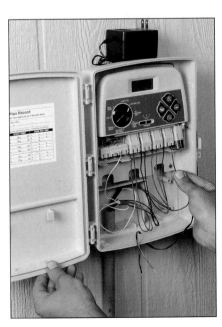

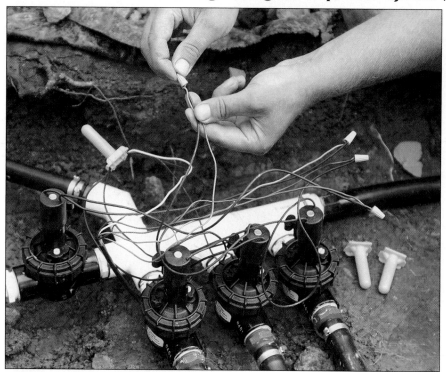

8 The valve manifold assembly is first hooked up to feeder tubing running out to each valve zone, then the wiring connections to the timer/control panel are made, using approved, multistrand, direct-burial underground wire. In the trenches, the wire is run beneath the tubing. All connections are then sealed with watertight gel cap protectors.

9 Once the valve manifold is plumbed and wired, it's buried in the valve cover box to protect it, while keeping it accessible.

10 The individual sprinkler heads are installed. First, the supply tubing is connected to the main supply tube, then trimmed to length with tubing cutters.

11 A 90° barbed coupling is inserted in the supply tubing for the sprinkler head.

12 The barbed coupling is attached to the supply hose with a hose clamp.

13 The riser tube that attaches to the sprinkler head is measured and cut to height.

14 Final connections are made between the riser tube, which is threaded into the barbed coupling, and the sprinkler head. Backfill is dumped around the head to hold it stationary.

15 Power and water supply are restored at the main shutoffs and the system is tested and flushed out with the sprinkler heads removed. Since there were no leaks and everything worked fine, the trenches and holes were covered and the job was complete.

Push reel mowers are a joy on smaller, flatter, lawns and a workout on large or hilly lawns. This old classic has charm, but high quality modern push reel mowers are lighter, lower in maintenance and more effective.

Mowing

Grass evolved with grazing animals and still depends upon regular cutting to stay healthy and thick. Attentive mowing promotes development of new grass and helps control certain weeds. Mowing too short can be just as much of a problem as not mowing frequently enough. Below are the five rules for proper mowing.

1. Mow high. Mow to the maximum recommended mowing height for your grass species (listed in "Grass Types," pages 34 to 46) when the grass is stressed. Stresses include drought, shade and emergence of annual weeds. Annual weeds germinate in the spring in the North and in the spring and late summer/early fall in the South. Certain creeping warm-season grasses, like bermudagrass, centipedegrass and carpetgrass, are kept competitive by short mowing. Last, it's a good idea to mow before weeds go to seed to prevent their spread.

2. Take one-third of the leaf blade at a mowing. This could mean weekly or more frequent mowing during high-growth periods for the faster growing grasses and much longer intervals between mowing when the grass is not growing fast or the species is a

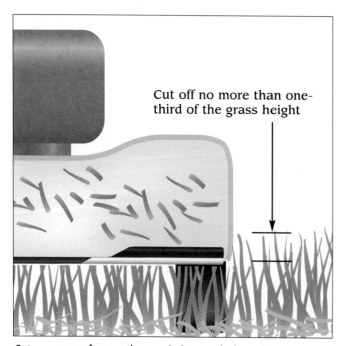

Cut off no more than one-third of the grass height

Cut your grass frequently enough that you don't need to remove more than ⅓ of the total plant height to trim it back into its recommended height range.

slow grower. Note that you'll mow less frequently when you cut grass high, since ⅓ of a longer blade takes more time to grow. Taking more than ⅓ of the leaf blade stresses the plant by reducing the supply of sugars to the roots and by exposing the previously shaded lower part of the plants to sunburn.

TIP: If your grass gets too high, mow at your highest mower setting on the first mowing, wait three days, then mow to the preferred height.

3. Leave grass clippings to rot, whether you use a mulching mower or not. You should not rake clippings or use a mower with a bag unless special circumstances exist. The clippings return nitrogen to the soil, reducing the need to fertilize; they add organic matter to the soil, which feeds valuable microorganisms and increases the resilience of the lawn to disease and drought. Contrary to popular belief, grass clippings do not contribute to thatch buildup. Remove and compost clippings if they contain many weed seed heads or rooting runners of weeds. Also, remove or disperse rows, piles or clumps of grass clippings.

4. Don't mow a wet lawn, as it leaves clumps of grass and can foster the spread of disease.

5. Keep your lawn mower blade sharp to prevent injury to grass and spread of disease. Sharp blades are critical on newly seeded grass, which may be uprooted by a dull rotary blade.

Mulching mowers speed up the decomposition of clippings in your lawn, serving the two-fold purpose of fertilizing and eliminating unsightly clipping clumps.

Never mow a wet lawn. It creates clumps of grass that are strewn throughout the yard, where they can damage living plants if left for more than a day; it leaves the cut grass very vulnerable to disease; it causes stress on your mower engine, and makes a mess of the mower deck, too.

A sharp blade does a neater job of mowing grass and is much less likely to damage the grass plants than a dull blade. See page 25.

Mower Safety

Danger: Please be careful with lawn mowers, which in sheer numbers of accidents are one of the most dangerous machines to users and bystanders. They can take the use of a hand, an eye or seriously injure or kill a child. Importantly:

1. Keep hands, feet, and clothing away from cutting blades.
2. Motor should be off and spark plug disconnected before attempting service that will put your hand near the blade.
3. Keep children inside when mowing.
4. Mow across slopes, not up and down.
5. Do not leave a running mower unattended.
6. Look down and behind before mowing backwards.
7. Remove objects from lawn before mowing and do not mow over gravel or stones.
8. Do not mow wet grass.
9. Mow sober and alert and wear shoes with good traction.

MORE MOWING TIPS

Power reel mowers can cut lower than rotary mowers without scalping because they conform to uneven ground. While rotary mowers can leave blade ends ragged and brown, reels produce an even scissor-action cut. Power reel mowers are by far the best tools for cutting hybrid bermudagrass, creeping bentgrass and St. Augustinegrass.

Generally, it's better not to bag lawn clippings; however, if the grass has become very long or if weed grasses and broadleafs are in seed, bag the clippings.

One of the advantages of owning a garden tractor is that you can find a host of useful accessories, from trailers, like the one shown above, to tillers, broadcast spreaders and even grading attachments.

Edging

Visually, humans focus on edges. Practically, this means that if you make the borders of your lawn sharp and clean, you can relax a little about imperfections in the middle. There are a number of tools out there that can help you maintain the lawn's edge on an ongoing basis. These include grass shears, long-handled edging shears, string trimmers, and manual rotary edgers that can be pushed along the edge. Use these whenever the grass starts creeping beyond the lawn area.

If your edge is allowed to run wild for a while, the more mild-mannered of these tools will not be able to pull the grass back, however. It's then that you'll want to rent a power edger to chop back the spreading grasses. For information on establishing a new edge or laying edging, see pages 130 to 131. For a tidy border effect, chop a clean vertical edge on the lawn and clip back any vegetation coming in the other direction from the garden. Don't be afraid to reach back under larger creeping plants like junipers to clip them closer to the source. That way all the cutting doesn't happen in a single plane.

Power edgers (available at most rental centers) make short work of badly overgrown lawn borders. A flat-edge spade also works well for cutting back sod to the edge of a paved surface.

A manual roll edger works for regularly maintained edges, but may meet its match on long-neglected lawn borders.

Create an unplanted area 6 to 12 in. wide between garden and lawn. As an added effect, lay mulch in the cleared area—this will help slow the invasion of grass, garden plants and weeds, and it will create a striking visual border.

Adjust the pH of acidic or alkaline soil to help control moss and other weeds. Correct pH also helps your grass grow better, controlling the weeds indirectly. Lime pellets and hydrated lime are applied to a lawn to help neutralize acidic soil.

Weeds & Weed Control

Weeds are a little bit like vegetables—you know one when you see one, but they tend to defy hard, scientific definitions. A weed to one person is a valued plant to somebody else, and may not even show up on the radar screen of yet a third person. But the only person whose opinion really matters is you. If there is a plant in your yard that you wish to get rid of, there are ample ways it can be accomplished.

But to editorialize for a moment, think twice before you automatically attack any intruding plant in your yard. Allowing a lawn to include non-grass plants does have some advantages. Ecological diversity in your

WEED OR NOT-WEED?
The case for clover

Ultimately, a weed is a plant you don't want. Clover, henbit, violets, daisies and other low-growing broadleaf plants may be weeds or turf plants, depending on your point of view. Pure grass lawns are more even, but mixtures of grass and other plants may be easier to maintain and more insect and disease resistant.

White clover fertilizes grass by fixing nitrogen from the air, and clover impedes the spread of grass diseases. But some don't like the rustic look of lawns with clover, its attraction to bees, or its tendency to stain clothes green when played on. Is clover a weed or turf plant? You decide.

White clover

yard makes disease and insect problems less likely. Many turf plants have low, attractive flowers and are more tolerant of poor soil, drought and neglect than grass. Finally, maintaining an all-grass lawn in an area that favors another plant type means that you will need to work that much harder to keep the grass there and the "weed" out.

However, keeping certain plants out, whether "weed" species of grass or non-grass plants, can make sense for aesthetic and practical reasons. Annual plants, whether grasses or non-grasses, die after one year, leaving ugly dead spots in the yard. Some plants send up large, ragged seed heads or spikes and others have coarse, unsightly leaves that break up the evenness of the turf. Finally, plants that spread aggressively when your main turf species are dormant can leave a lawn patchy and uneven when the invader is dormant.

Decide for yourself which and how many non-turf grass plants you will tolerate before establishing a weed control regimen. Determine if a particular plant is adding to your dissatisfaction with your lawn, or if the weed is incidental to larger lawn-health problems that could be mitigated with a better watering, fertilizing, composting, aerating or dethatching program.

Weed Control

Turf grasses are naturally aggressive, and if the conditions are right, they will out-compete other plants. Below are cultural practices that favor grass over weeds.

Keep grass the right height. Regular mowing controls taller perennial weeds and keeps weeds from seeding. But mowing high when you do mow helps many grasses out-compete germinating weeds. Tall grass will smother the competition from newly germinating annual weeds. Higher mowing in shade and during dry periods also give these grasses an advantage over weeds. Low creeping grasses like bermudagrass, centipedegrass and creeping bentgrass usually don't benefit from high mowing.

Nitrogen fertilizer generally benefits grass more than broadleaf plants, helping your grass win the battle for turf. Do not add fertilizer when the weeds will benefit more than the grass, such as when warm-season grasses are dormant in the fall and winter or cool-season grasses are dormant in the summer. Adding too much fertilizer can damage the soil and the grass, opening up a window for weeds that tolerate compaction and fertilizer salts. See pages 70 to 75 for more information on the correct timing and application of fertilizers.

Provide drainage for waterlogged soils, provide aeration for compacted soils, and provide a path in soils that undergo heavy foot traffic. Alternately, switch to a grass species that will tolerate your existing soil conditions.

Give grass a competitive edge. Thin out crowded trees and tree branches to allow underlying grass to out-compete shade- and dry-soil-tolerant weeds. Even so-called "shade tolerant" grasses need some sun. Plus, tree roots draw a lot of water from the soil.

Tall Grass As Weed Control

Studies at the University of Rhode Island found that after five years there was more than 700% more crabgrass in plots that were mowed to 1¼ in. than in plots that were mowed to 2¼ in. At the University of Maryland, scientists found almost seven times as many kinds of weeds in a plot mowed to 1½ in. than in a plot mowed to 2½ in.

Direct weed control methods

Direct weed control is the process of taking your battle right to the weed, through a variety of methods, rather than attempting to resolve the underlying reasons for the weed's presence. It is sometimes the only alternative if invading plants are on the verge of becoming established. In the long run, you'll need to implement the cultural fixes that will make the lawn environment less hospitable for weeds.

There are basically two ways to attack a weed directly: dig it out, or kill it with herbicide. Once the weeds are gone, look into aerating, dethatching, sensible fertilizing, and proper watering as long-term cures to keep them at bay so your turf grasses can thrive.

Use a dandelion digger or other appropriate weeding tool to remove deep-rooted perennial weeds by hand. This is best done a day after rain or a thorough watering, when the soil is soft. Get as much of the root as possible, since large pieces of tap root will come back more often and with more vigor than small pieces will.

CONTROLLING WEEDS BY HAND

Rake and mow early in the season before spreading weeds get the upper hand. Weeds like ground ivy (Creeping Charlie to some) and perennial speedwell can have their rooting stems dislodged from the ground with a thatch rake or a stiff garden rake. Mow low after raking, then rake up and dispose of the stems (severed stems can re-root).

Specially designed weeding tools like this dandelion digger can get deep into the soil and slice the weed root, leaving virtually no tap root behind to reestablish.

Preemergent herbicide

Preemergent herbicides kill broadleaf and grass weeds (like crabgrass) just as they are germinating from seed. If the weed is already growing, preemergent herbicides will not work, and they will not control perennial weeds coming back from established roots and rhizomes. Apply in early spring. In the South, preemergent herbicides may also be spread in the late summer or early fall, before winter weeds germinate. Identify your grass species (See pages 34 to 36) and check herbicide labels for grass sensitivities. Even "non-sensitive" grasses can be injured by herbicides if they are stressed by drought. Most herbicides should not be applied to new lawns, though siduron and simazine are two preemergent herbicides that control crabgrass in new lawns. Carefully follow the container instructions when applying preemergents. They should be watered in after application. Be extremely careful to sweep up any herbicide that spills onto pavement. Keep pets and children off treated areas for the specified amount of time.

Postemergent herbicide

Postemergent herbicides for lawns usually contain 2,4-D and related chemicals that kill broadleaf plants such as dandelions, clover and chickweed, but don't harm grass or grass-like weeds. The spray-on kind work much better against the weeds than granular postemergent herbicides, but sprays pose a real risk to the environment from drift and the most common ones have known toxicity to humans and animals. Instead of broadly spraying these herbicides with a hose-end sprayer, spot-apply smaller quantities with a tank sprayer or a ready-mixed sprayer. That way, you can target weeds without risk of damaging non-target plants, like ornamental trees and perennials. Spot-application is also safer for children, pets and the environment, since not as much product is applied. Apply postemergent herbicides when soil moisture is plentiful, weeds are actively growing and temperatures are below 90°. Weeds are particularly vulnerable after they're done flowering but before they go dormant in late summer or early fall. At this time, sugars are traveling from leaves to root and the herbicide can hitch a ride. Bentgrass, St. Augustinegrass, and centipedegrass may be injured by postemergent herbicides for broadleaf weeds.

Apply postemergent, spot weed killers for broadleafs when soil moisture is plentiful and weeds are growing vigorously. Avoid spraying in very hot weather and before rain. Wear protective clothing when spraying and keep pets and children away for the recommended time. Products for broadleafs do not kill grass weeds, but some turf grasses may be slightly injured by these herbicides.

Common Weeds & How to Control Them

Weeds are divided roughly into categories: broadleaf or grass, perennial or annual, and warm-season or cool-season. This gives you eight possible categories in which a weed can fall (e.g. cool-season broadleaf annual, cool-season broadleaf perennial, warm-season broadleaf annual, etc...). Even if you just figure out what category your problem weed falls into, you're a long way toward figuring out how to control it. That's because weed control depends heavily on these variables. Weeds also tell you when something is wrong with your lawn. You may kill the messenger, but if you don't address the underlying problem, the health of your turf grass will not improve and weeds will invade again. Below we look at some representative weeds from each of the categories, see how they are best controlled, and look at underlying conditions that may have allowed these weeds to become established to begin with.

What's wrong with weed-and-feed products?

Preemergent weed-and-feed products for the spring have a timing problem. The preemergent needs to be applied early, before the weed seeds germinate. Fertilizing grass at this time can over-stimulate top growth, making the grass susceptible to disease and a late frost damage.

The timing of postemergent weed-and-feed products is perfect when used in the early fall on cool-season grasses, but they have a delivery problem. Granular products do a poor job of coating leaves with herbicide, thus granular weed-and-feed products with postemergent herbicides are not very effective.

Defining Weed Categories

Grasses: The grass family is huge and includes many important flowering plants including sugarcane, bamboo, corn, wheat and rice. All emerge from the ground as a single cotyledon (they are "monocots") and all have parallel-veined and relatively long narrow leaves. Grasses are distinguished from broadleaf plants for weed control because certain classes of herbicides kill grasses and others kill broadleaf plants. That's why it's possible to broadcast some post-emergent herbicides over the whole lawn and have only the broadleaf plants die.

Broadleaf Plants: Broadleafs include many families of flowering plants. All emerge from the ground as two cotyledons, which is why broadleaf plants are called "dicots." Leaves on broadleaf plants have veins that branch from a single point or off a central rib. Broadleaf plants include most trees, bushes and annual and perennial plants, but not things that look like grass, such as tulips, daffodils, onions and irises. Some broadleaf plants, like dandelions, don't have very broad leaves, but if you examine their leaves, you will see the branching vein pattern that puts them in the group.

Perennials: Perennial plants live from year to year. Herbaceous perennials, like the kind that become weeds in lawns, die down to the ground each year but store carbohydrates for next year's growth in swollen underground roots, rhizomes, corms and bulbs. Whether monocots or broadleaf plants, perennials often survive when cut down to the ground since they grow from underground buds.

Annuals: Annuals die after a season of growth, but before they do, they put all their energy into producing as many seeds as they can. Some annuals, like lambsquarters, can produce more than one million seeds per plant. Mowing your grass high keeps annual species under control because it leaves no room for the delicate young plants to sprout and grow. Preemergent herbicides work well against annuals because they prevent seeds from germinating—the only way an annual can carry on from year to year.

Warm-season and Cool-season Plants: All of the plants discussed above may be either a warm-season or a cool-season plant. Warm-season plants like bermudagrass do most of their growing in the summer when soil temperatures are over 70°F. Cool-season plants grow better in cool fall and spring weather. They even grow in the winter in the South.

Cool-season perennials are a tough class of weeds from North to South. They weather cold winters and hot summers with reserves stored underground, and come on strong in spring and fall (and winter in the South). Many of the broadleafs of this category stay close to the ground and root as they spread. It's best to catch these early in the spring—raking up the runners, mowing low and removing the debris, which could otherwise re-root. The grasses of this category need to be dug up or spot-killed with herbicide specifically formulated for grass weeds or all weeds (herbicides that can also kill your turfgrass). Do not fertilize and water in the cooler parts of the year in the South if you have a cool-season weed problem.

Cool-season Perennial Grass & Grass-like Weeds:

Quackgrass. *Agropyron repens.*

The wide, coarse leaves of this perennial can grow up to three feet high if unmown. Quackgrass spreads by long, fast-growing, white rhizomes and may turn brown in summer. Keep grass mowed and fertilized to help crowd out quackgrass. Chop into the runners with a spade. Spot-treat with a non-selective herbicide like glyphosate, but realize that this will also kill lawn grass.

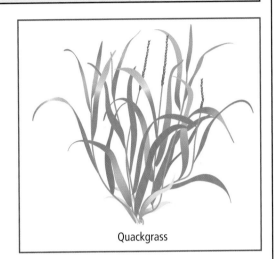

Quackgrass

Wild garlic and onion. *Allium vineale and A. canadense.*

Early to green in the spring, these weeds have hollow (garlic) or solid (onion), narrow round leaves that smell like onions and garlic when crushed. An early low mowing before the grass has started to grow will remove old dead grass tips, knock back the onions and garlic, and prevent these from spreading by seed, which develop from purple and white flowers on the tops. (Garlic also forms bulblets.) To eliminate these plants, their bulbs must be dug up or a broad-spectrum herbicide containing glyphosate or a spot-weeder that controls this genus must be applied to each plant when they are growing in early spring. Late fall herbicide applications are also effective since sugars from the leaves are being transported to the bulbs and the herbicide can hitch a ride. Avoid getting these herbicides on your lawn grass.

Wild Garlic

Cool-season Perennial Broad-leaf Weeds:

Canada Thistle. *Cirsium arvense.*

Leaves are lobed with margins prickling with spines. Numerous purple or white composite flowers are borne on one- to five-foot-tall stems that branch near the top. A network of roots sends up new shoots around one established plant, creating dense clumps of thistles, which are very difficult to eradicate. Eliminate by pulling the plants or by regularly treating them with a spot herbicide. Complete elimination can take years. Keep a lawn with thistle well mowed; never allow the plant to go to seed. They usually establish in lawns that have been allowed to get too long and sparse.

Canada Thistle

Cool-season Perennial Broadleaf Weeds (cont.):

Dandelion. *Taraxacum officinale.*

Dandelion

A low rosette of basal leaves lets dandelions survive the mower, and a puffball of parachuted seeds after spring and fall blooming keeps the species colonizing new turf. But contrary to popular belief, dandelion is not the toughest weed on the planet. A little persistence with any of the control methods outlined below will eliminate dandelions from a healthy lawn.

Method 1) When dandelions are blooming, their root reserves of carbohydrate are at their lowest. Dig as much of the root out as you can at this time with a dandelion weeder, weed popper or any other tool designed to uproot tap-rooted weeds. Try to get at least 4 or 5 in. of root. The remaining root tip will rarely have enough energy to send up another plant.

Method 2) Use long-handled shears to cut the dandelion leaves and stem off as low as possible. Do this repeatedly, perhaps 5 or 6 times during the growing season, and the roots will run out of energy.

Method 3) Spot-treat dandelions with an herbicide advertised to kill dandelions. Herbicides are most effective on dandelions before blooming in early spring and again in late summer or early fall, when the leaves are sending starches to the root.

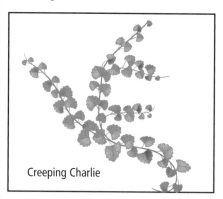
Creeping Charlie

Ground Ivy, Creeping Charlie. *Glechoma hederacea.*

This mint blooms in late spring and early summer and has the square stem and trumpet-like, two-lipped purple flowers typical of the family. Round, deeply veined, scalloped-edged leaves are opposite each other on the stem. The plant spreads rapidly with running stems that can root where they contact soil. Control is most effective in early spring, before the plants have gotten too big. Use a garden rake to uproot the runners, then mow the plants close for control, or pull them up to eliminate. Either way, make sure you rake up the stems so they don't root again. Ground ivy responds slowly to spot treatment of herbicides.

Plantain. *Plantago major.*

Broad leaves grow in a rosette from a ground-level growing point that also sends up narrow spikes of inconspicuous flowers that become seeds. Plantain likes thin grass and compacted soil. Aerating, adding compost, and fertilizing can all help a struggling turf grass overcome plantain. Dig plantain up by the root to remove.

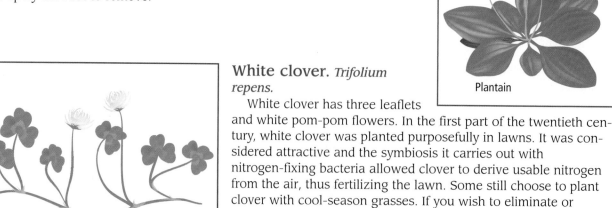
Plantain

White Clover

White clover. *Trifolium repens.*

White clover has three leaflets and white pom-pom flowers. In the first part of the twentieth century, white clover was planted purposefully in lawns. It was considered attractive and the symbiosis it carries out with nitrogen-fixing bacteria allowed clover to derive usable nitrogen from the air, thus fertilizing the lawn. Some still choose to plant clover with cool-season grasses. If you wish to eliminate or reduce your clover, increase nitrogen fertilizer rates and reduce phosphorous fertilization to give grass the competitive edge.

Many cool-season annuals are not considered weeds by northern lawnsmiths. In the south, cool-season annual weeds germinate and grow in the fall, winter and spring, making brown, winter lawns look particularly unkempt. Southern lawn owners can fight annual weeds by mowing turf grasses high in the late summer and fall, which discourages the germination of cool-season weeds. This only works with tall grasses like bahiagrass and St. Augustinegrass. Otherwise, overseed with annual or perennial ryegrass in the fall for a green mowable winter lawn. Prevent the germination of cool-season annuals in the South with an application of preemergent granular herbicide in late summer and early spring.

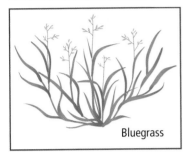

Bluegrass

Annual bluegrass. *Poa annua.*

This annual resembles perennial bluegrass but goes to seed more quickly, giving lawns a whitish cast. Annual bluegrass usually turns brown in the summer, causing northern owners to suspect disease. This grass likes compacted, moist soils. Aerate the soil and mow with the blade high to smother annual bluegrass, but mow often to keep seeds from forming. Remove the grass by pulling. Control in the winter in the South by overseeding with an annual rye.

Common Chickweed. *Stellaria media.*

Chickweed is a low annual with small, smooth, pointed leaves and small white flowers that bloom almost continuously. Seeds germinate in late fall and early spring. Chickweed spreads with rooting branches on wet, shady, or too frequently watered lawns. Pull or cut chickweed and rake up the stems, which can continue to ripen seeds even when uprooted.

Chickweed

Henbit. *Lamium amplexicaule.*

Henbit

Square stems give henbit away as a member of the mint family. Opposite-paired, roundish, ruffled leaves clasp the stem and are stalkless near the tops of upturned stems, though the lowest leaves have long stalks. Purple flowers are trumpet-shaped. Henbit grows on new or thin lawns in soils that are rich and well watered, and it grows as a vigorous winter annual in the South. Before seeding a new lawn, eliminate henbit with a season of regular tillage or herbicide application. In established lawns, pull henbit and correct fertility, drainage or aeration problems that are keeping the grass from filling in thickly. In the South, vigorous, thick grass mown high in late summer and early fall will discourage fall germination of henbit.

Prostrate Knotweed. *Polygonum aviculare.*

Wiry stems spread from a central taproot and form a mat of foliage, but the branches do not root. Tiny white flowers emerge at the base of oblong leaves. Knotweed appears in early spring on compacted soils, looking like grass at first. Knotweed can be pulled, cut back, or spot-killed with an herbicide at the three-leaf stage in mid to late spring. Correct the pavement-like conditions that favor knotweed by aerating the soil and adding compost.

Knotweed

Black Medic. *Medicago lupulina.*

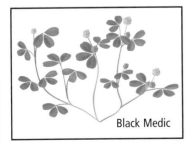

Black Medic

The three-leaflet clover-like leaves of medic have shallow teeth at the tips of the leaflets, and center leaflets that sit on a little stalk. The yellow flowers give rise to kidney-shaped, one-seeded pods that become black with age. Like clover, medic derives its own nitrogen from the air with the help of a symbiotic bacteria. This puts them at an advantage on nitrogen-poor soils. Applying compost and nitrogen fertilizer and reducing or eliminating phosphorous fertilizer will help grass get the upper hand.

The bane of the North, warm-season annual weeds thrive under conditions unwittingly created by many cool-season lawn enthusiasts. Frequent shallow watering favors their germination and shallow-rooted growth. Summer fertilization keeps them growing when cool-season grasses are too hot and dry to put up a fight. Southern lawn owners may find themselves up against warm-season broadleaf weeds on thin grass over poor or dry soils. Compacted soils from heavy traffic make life difficult for deep-rooted perennials, letting these undesirable annuals jump into the openings. The best way to control warm-season annuals is by fertilizing at the appropriate times, watering infrequently but deeply, aerating compacted soils, mowing high, and by pulling the offending weeds and removing clippings when these plants are in seed. Below are a sampling of the weeds, what they tell you about your lawn, and what you can do to control them.

Warm-season Annual Grass Weeds:

Crabgrass. *Digitaria ischaemum and D. sanguinalis.*

These light-green, annual grasses with prostrate stems and short hairy leaves can take over thin cool-season lawns when the turf grasses slow down in the summer. The spreading plants will root at the stem nodes, expanding "crablike." Setting the mower high and fertilizing at the right time allows turf grass to take control in one to five seasons. Mow high in the spring and summer. Fertilize cool-season grasses once in the fall, twice in the fall, or twice in the fall and once in late spring, but never in the summer.

Crabgrass

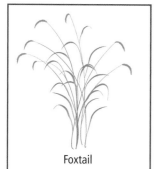
Foxtail

Foxtail (green and yellow). *Setaria viridis and S. glauca.*

Green foxtail has hairy leaf tops. Both green and yellow foxtail produce dense, bristly seed heads. Mow the lawn high and avoid summer fertilization on northern lawns. Dig up plants and remove clippings when the foxtail is in seed. Foxtails can indicate a need for soil aeration and compost, which will favor your turf grass over foxtail.

Sandbur. *Cenchrus pauciflorus.*

Sandbur is a low spreading annual grass with spiked seed burrs. It does best on poor sandy soil, so if you've got it, it's probably not your only problem. Rake half an inch of a fine compost or composted manure into your lawn every year until your thickened turf grass drowns out the sandbur. Mow high.

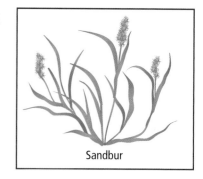
Sandbur

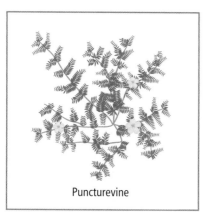
Puncturevine

Warm-season Annual Broadleaf Weeds:

Puncturevine. *Tribulus terrestris.*

Prostrate branching stems spread up to 5 ft. Two-inch-long leaves are hairy and divided into tiny leaflets along a central rib. Yellow flowers in summer turn to sharp-spined seedpods from July into fall. This is mainly a southern weed on poor compacted soils. Eliminate puncturevine by digging and by spot applications of herbicide, but more importantly, by aerating your soil, topdressing with compost, and by keeping off your lawn when it's wet and you're likely to cause soil compaction.

Warm-season Annual Broadleaf Weeds (cont.):

Purslane. *Portulaca oleracea.*

Thick, reddish stems with small oblong or egg-shaped fleshy leaves spread low over dry ground. Small yellow flowers turn to pods full of small black seeds in summer. The sap of this plant is clear. Purslane tolerates dry, hot soils and readily invades new or thin grass. Pull and remove plants, which will re-root if left in place. Regular deep watering of new grass will favor your turf over purslane.

Purslane

Spurges. *Euphorbia maculata and E. supine.*

These spurges (spotted and prostrate), a relative of the poinsettia, are found in lawns and in the cracks of sidewalks as very flat plants, with low stems that radiate out from a central tap root. Tiny pale pink or white flowers grow at the bases of small, smooth, oval leaves that may be tinted red or have reddish spots. If you break the stem, milky fluid will come out. Spurges are found in thin, drought-stressed northern lawns. Deep, regular irrigation, the addition of compost and fall fertilization will help keep lawns free of spurges.

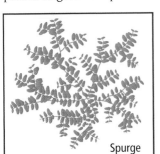

Spurge

Warm-season perennials are those overgrown, sometimes creeping, things with lots of roots that come back in the same place, in the heat of the summer, year in and year out. Most of them are grasses or grass-like. Though they are tough, they create more headaches when pampered in summer, especially in cool-season lawns where the desirable grasses can't benefit from summer fertilization due to heat. To control, fertilize and water in spring and fall, not in the summer, and mow high in summer. If you do water in the summer, water deeply and infrequently. Dig up warm-season perennials by hand and reseed or sod with your grass species. Many of the warm-season weeds are themselves warm-season turf grasses out of place in northern lawns.

Yellow nutsedge. *Cyperus esculentus.*

Nutsedge has triangular stems, a sure giveaway that it's a sedge and not a grass. The leaves are light green to yellow. Nutsedge has shallow roots and doesn't like dry soil, so water infrequently and deeply in the summer. High mowing also gives your grass an advantage over sedge.

Bermudagrass. *Cynodon dactylon.*

(See page 36 for identification information.) Bermudagrass spreads underground by rhizome and above ground by stolons and can take over cool-season lawns during summer in the transition zone. As a warm-season grass, it will turn brown in the winter. Bermudagrass tolerates compacted soils and likes high fertility, so fertilize only in the fall to help your cool-season turf win out, and while you're at it, aerate the soil. For serious infestations, you can kill bermudagrass with Roundup, Kleenup, or some other glyphosate-containing herbicide and then plant a new cool-season lawn in the fall, preferably with a more competitive species. Warning: leave a month or more to kill off bermudagrass; you'll probably need repeated applications.

Yellow Nutsedge

Zoysiagrass. *Zoysia japonica.*

(See page 38 for identification information.) Zoysia is more cold-hardy than other southern turf grasses, and so makes a natural weed in cool-season grasses as far north as southern New England. Zoysiagrass spreads by stolons and rhizomes and tolerates traffic. It browns out in fall until warm weather returns in midspring. To contain, avoid summer watering and fertilization. To eliminate, kill it with repeated applications of glyphosate or dig up zoysiagrass and reseed a cool-season grass in the fall.

Pest Control

Insects that eat grass (caterpillar worms) or that suck juices from grass (chinch bugs, aphids) can be identified by the "soapy water test." Take a large coffee can, cut off both ends, and twist one side an inch or two into the ground, cutting away grass that gets in the way with a knife. Fill the can with water with a squirt of dish soap mixed in it. Keep water in the can for five minutes, re-filling if needed. The irritated bugs will let go and float during that time.

Sod pest exam

To find root-feeding bugs, such as white grubs and the grubs of billbugs, pull back a piece of sod that's 2 in. thick and 1 sq. ft. in size. Sift through the soil beneath. Replace and water the sod afterwards.

Insects can damage lawns, but it's not always clear which insect, if any, is to blame when lawn problems crop up. All pest insects may exist in lawns at levels below the threshold at which they do real damage. You may be inclined to spray and hope for the best, but there are some good reasons not to do this. For every one organism that's a problem, there are hundreds that in some way benefit the lawn, either by breaking down thatch and clippings, by recycling nutrients and aerating the soil, or by feeding on fungi and insects harmful to the grass. If you spray a chemical that's toxic to many things in the lawn, you can end up with more problems than you started with. Good turf grass managers approach insect control in the following order:

1. Focus first on growing healthy grass that will resist insects. Importantly, try to develop a deep-rooted, slow-growing grass using the techniques of deep, infrequent watering and "just-enough" fertilization described in this chapter. Keep soil dethatched and aerated and adjust pH problems and mineral deficiencies according to the recommendations of a soil-testing laboratory.

2. Identify insect problems correctly and react appropriately. Pest insects are only pests if they exist in your lawn above a certain density. Spraying insecticides brings on the possibility that insects that feed on pests or perform other vital functions in the grass community will be killed by the spray.

3. Use biological controls whenever possible. These "natural" control methods often persist as long as the pest persists, providing ongoing control without the risk of killing non-target organisms. Biological controls include application of bacteria, nematodes and fungi, as well as the feeding habits of birds and insects that may be attracted to your property with border plantings.

Looking for insects

Look for insects that may be causing your problems on the edges of damaged grass, or in undamaged or partly damaged grass. If dead grass has bugs, they probably didn't cause the problem, since bugs that harm living grass need to be near living grass.

Agents for Insect Control

Biological controls

Biological controls are living organisms that attack pests. They usually act more slowly than chemical or botanical controls, but some persist in the environment, effecting control for years to come. Usually, the earlier in the lifecycle of an insect you apply a biological control, the more effective it will be. Most biological controls are very specific, not harming beneficial organisms.

Examples:

Bacillus thuringiensis (Bt) is a bacterium that produces protein crystals that interfere with the digestion of caterpillars and many other insects. Make sure to buy Bt bred to kill the pest you are trying to eliminate. Bt's don't harm most beneficial insects and are very safe to use. Bt is mixed with water and sprayed. It sells under the trade names *BT, Bactospeine, Caterpillar Attack, Dipel, Javelin, Condor T/O* and more.

Bacillus popillae (Milky Spore) is a bacterium that must be alive to work. It's used most effectively against the grubs of Japanese beetles. For best effect, everybody in an area must use it, and it must be used repeatedly. Milky spore is safe for people and pets. It's sold under the names *Japademic* and *Doom.*

Beauveria bassiana (white fungus) is a fungus that's used against grubs, caterpillar worms, chinch bugs and billbugs. It's very safe for humans and pets. It sells under the name Naturalis-T and others.

Predatory nematodes are very small, wormlike organisms including *Heterorhabditis bacteriophora* and *Steinernema glaseri.* They attack the larval stages of hundreds of insect pests; make sure the species you buy specifies your pest. Nematodes are applied living, so they must be fresh and protected from heat. Water them in well for maximum effectiveness. They sell under the names *Exhibit, Vector, Cruiser, Scanmask* and others.

Insecticidal Soaps

Insecticidal soaps kill small bugs like mites, scale and aphids. Unless the label states otherwise, insecticidal soaps contain soap only and are very safe. It's common now to find insecticidal soaps mixed with other relatively benign insecticides, like *Neem.*

Biological controls for pest problems are naturally occurring agents, including bacteria, fungi and proteins, that are packaged for deployment into problem areas.

Insecticidal soap is an environmentally safe product that's sprayed onto infested areas of plants to wash the infestation away. Some insecticides contain insecticidal soap as an additive.

Botanical Insecticides

Botanical insecticides should not be confused with biological controls. They contain no living agents, but act on target organisms chemically, like any other pesticide. They include pyrethrum, which is made from African chrysanthemums and contains pyrethrins as the active ingredients; *neem* (examples of products include *Margosan-O)*, which is made from the neem tree; sabadilla, which is made from plants in the lily family; and Rotenone, which is derived from several tropical plants. Many favor botanical insecticides because they don't persist in the environment and they don't usually harm people and other mammals. However, avoid pyrethrum and rotenone if you can use something else; these will kill many of the beneficial organisms as well as pests. Both pyrethrum and rotenone will also kill fish.

Diatomaceous Earth

Diatomaceous earth (photo, right) is made from the ancient shells of ocean-dwelling microorganisms. It pierces the armor of adult insects with microscopic points, and this causes the insects to dry up. Diatomaceous earth is most effective if applied in dry weather when the target insects, like billbugs, are moving around above ground. Diatomaceous earth is applied as a fine white powder. It is chemically inert and harmless if touched or swallowed, but avoid breathing in the dust.

Fighting insects with birds

Before chemical pesticides were big, the USDA researched and successfully demonstrated the use of birds to control insect problems in agriculture. Some birds eat lots of bugs, and they have to eat every day, so if you can attract the right birds to your property, they will reward you by controlling your problem bugs. To attract birds, plant trees, shrubs and other vegetation that the desired birds live and feed in (when they're not eating your bugs). Birdhouses may also be used to attract predatory birds. Below are some examples of vegetation associated with birds that eat insects that feed on grass and grass roots.

Northeast: balsam fir, birch, blackberry, cherry (wild), dogwood, flower gardens, hemlock, hop hornbeam, huckleberry, native grasses and weeds, oak, pine, spruce.

Southeast: black gum, (native) fruit-bearing trees, shrubs, brambles, vines, tall grasses and weeds, oak, pine.

Southwest: alfilaria (filaree), dogwood, elderberry, evergreens generally, hackberry, honeysuckle, juniper, native fruit bearers, native grasses and weeds, native underbrush, oak, pines, pinyon, shade trees generally.

Northwest: alfilaria (filaree), cedar, dogwood, elderberry, grape, hemlock, native grasses and weeds, oak, pine, raspberries.

Midwest: cedar, conifers generally, dogwood, hackberry, hawthorn, huckleberry, native flower gardens, native fruit bearers, native grasses and weeds, oak, pine.

Ladybugs eat aphids, mites, and scale insects. Use of some pesticides will kill ladybugs and other predators. Since one predatory insect eats many harmful pests, spraying can sometimes worsen pest problems.

Fighting insects with insects

Beneficial insects eat other insects that feed on the roots and leaves of grass. Many plants give alternate sources of food to these insects, which increases their numbers and encourages them to hunt for protein in your lawn. In particular, plant herbs and ornamentals that flower in umbrels or have composite flowers. Umbrel plants include Queen Anne's lace, parsley, caraway, fennel and dill. Composites include Black-eyed Susans, sunflowers, straw flowers, yarrow and daisies.

Fighting insects with a dethatcher

Dethatching eliminates thatch—the habitat of many pests. Thatch also absorbs pesticides and anything else you put on the lawn, protecting the target organisms. Before spraying anything, remove the thatch layer with a verticutter or power rake.

Caterpillar Worms

Caterpillar worms are the larval form of moths and butterflies. They may be sleek and striped or thick and hairless. Caterpillar worms chew off the grass blades just above the thatch line, leaving patches of scalped lawn in their wake. Look for silky tubes, fuzz-covered eggs, or silky webs near the soil surface. Use the can and soapy water method (page 106) at the edge of damaged grass to flush them out.

Control:

Use a power rake or verticutter to remove a thatch layer and reduce habitat of the worms and make anything you spray more effective.

Method 1, Biological: Late in the day, mow the lawn and spray the grass with Bt or parasitic nematodes produced specifically for caterpillar control. You can also use *Beauveria bassiana JW-1* against armyworms and sod webworms.

Method 2, Botanical: Sabadilla dust and/or neem-containing products (such as *Margosan-O*) will work if sprayed at the right time. Contact your county Cooperative Extension Service for timing and to find out what biological controls or pesticides are effective for the worms in your area.

Method 3, Prevention: Replant or overseed your lawn with endophyte-containing ryegrass (*Nobility, Repel, Delaware Dwarf*) and fescue varieties (*Finesse, and Focus*).

Long term: Attract predatory birds. They love to eat caterpillars.

Three common caterpillar worms:

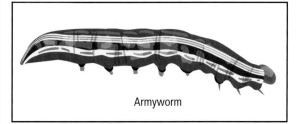

Armyworm

Armyworm

Armyworms, the larvae of dark-winged moths, lay fuzz-covered clusters of one hundred eggs or more at night on southern turf grasses. The larvae emerge white with black heads and grow to 1½-in.-long caterpillars in a month or less. More mature larvae are green or greenish brown with three lighter stripes running down their backs and sides. Armyworms can decimate southern lawns in the spring and fall. More than 5 per square yard may be a problem in turf.

Cutworm

Cutworms are big (up to 2 in.), smooth and come in different shades, specklings, and stripings of gray, black and brown. They metamorphize into night-flying moths. They curl up when disturbed. Cutworms will chew off grass blades at the base, especially in new lawns. More than 10 in a square foot is considered a problem in turf.

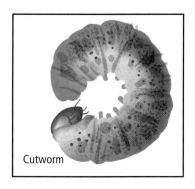

Cutworm

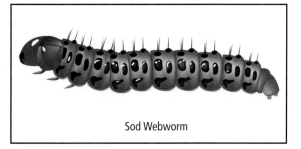

Sod Webworm

Sod Webworm

Sod Webworms are usually gray with black spots and reach ¾ in. long. They feed at night and on cloudy days and hide in a little silk tube in the thatch or ground during the day. The moths are buff-colored and appear narrow and with a little snout when stationary. They make short, erratic flights over the grass while laying their eggs at dusk. New generations of worms hatch and mature throughout the summer. Fifteen or more per square foot is considered a problem in turf.

White Grubs

White grubs, the larval stage of beetles, feed mostly on roots of cool-season grasses. They are thick, blunt and milky white, measure from ¼ to 1½ in. long, and are usually curled in a "C" shape. Their heads are yellow or brown, and they have three pairs of small legs and a massive abdomen. Grubs attract other animals, like moles and birds.

Grass may wilt (despite adequate water) and turf may become spongy and eventually yellow or brown when grubs are feeding. You may be able to pull back the sod like a rug, since the roots are attacked, and search out the grubs. Otherwise, cut and pull back a sample for inspection (See page 109). More than 5 grubs in a square foot suggest grubs are your problem.

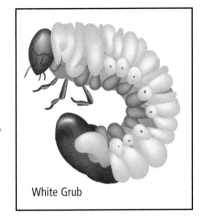

White Grub

Control:

Method 1: Turn badly infected areas repeatedly for a season. The birds will feast on the exposed larvae.

Method 2: Remove thatch and spray grubacides like neem, or biological controls like parasitic nematodes, *Beauveria bassiana*, and, for Japanese beetle grubs, milky spore. Timely spraying is critical so call your local Cooperative Extension Service agent to find out when to spray for grubs in your area. Irrigate dry soil thoroughly before spraying to bring grubs closer to the surface. Irrigate after applying pesticides to carry the pesticide or bio-control down in the soil.

Method 3: Pick adult beetles and drop them into a bucket of water with a thin layer of kerosene on top. Note: Traps don't work very well for residential-size lawns, since they attract beetles to your property.

Billbugs

Billbug

Billbug weevil adults are ¼ to ½ in. long and have a long snout (bill). The larvae are white with an orangish brown head and are about the size of puffed rice. Adults over-winter and lay eggs in the spring, and their larvae feed on surface stems in late spring, moving down to the roots and rhizomes as the temperatures rise. They pupate in late summer and emerge as a new batch of adults. Billbugs like bluegrass, bermudagrass and zoysiagrass. Look for adults and new larvae and the "sawdust" remaining from their feast on the edges of brown spots in spring. Look for larvae under the sod as you would for grubs (see above). One adult in spring or 10 larvae anytime per square foot is a problem.

Control:
Method 1: Increase mowing height to lower temperatures near soil. Aerate compacted soil and remove a thatch layer. Top-dress with compost to further cool the soil. Water deeply in the spring to encourage deep rooting.

Method 2: Control adults in the spring. Dethatch, if needed, then apply *neem* products or diatomaceous earth. Timing is critical. Contact your local Cooperative Extension Service for application timing.

Method 3: Dethatch if needed in late spring or early summer when pest is in larval form, and apply parasitic nematodes or *Beauveria bassiana JW-1* fungal spores. Water in agent thoroughly. Control becomes difficult as the larvae move down in the soil as the season progresses.

Method 4: Attract predators. Big-eyed bugs, hunting wasps, wrens, nuthatches and bluebirds eat billbugs and other weevils.

Method 5: Replant or overseed with resistant grasses, which include ryegrass and tall fescue varieties that contain endophytes and Kentucky bluegrass varieties that are labeled as resistant to billbugs.

Chinch Bug

Chinch Bugs

A chinch bug starts as a red nymph the size of a pinhead, with a white line across its back. Subsequent nymphs look more like the adult pictured and grow from 1/16 to 1/4 in. long. They're orange-brown to black, with white wings that have a dark angular spot on each. Chinch bugs turn grass yellow and brown by sucking out juices from leaves. The bugs smell terrible when crushed. Use the floatation method (See page 106) to count adults and nymphs. More than 20 in a square foot are a problem. Kentucky bluegrass, bentgrass, the fine fescues, St. Augustinegrass and zoysiagrass are most affected by chinch bugs.

Control:

Method 1: Increase mowing height to make the lawn more humid and cooler at soil level and dethatch to decrease habitat. Reduce nitrogen fertilizer to make the blades less succulent and to reduce thatch formation. Water more to help the grass survive infestation.

Method 2: Treat with white fungus *(Beauveria bassiana JW-1)* or *Heterorhabditis bacteriophora* nematodes. Sabadilla dust may be used to kill the bugs and larvae.

Method 3: Plant resistant grasses like *Floratam* St. Augustinegrass.

Mole Crickets

Mole crickets grow to 1 1/4 to 1 1/2 in. long as adults and have shovel-like forelegs that allow them to burrow. The nymphs look like little adults in early spring. Mole crickets damage southern lawns—particularly of bahiagrass, bermudagrass and centipedegrass—by digging shallow tunnels while feeding on roots. The grass above the tunnels dries out. Since you want to control mole crickets before they get big enough to make visible tunnels, use the can and soapy water method (page 106) to see how many nymphs you have. An average of 2 or 3 per square foot merits treatment.

Mole Cricket

Control:

Method 1: Spread *Beauveria bassiana JW-1* fungus or predatory nematodes.

Method 2: If you've pursued a high management approach to lawn care, try benign neglect. Fire ants, ground beetles, earwigs and spiders feed on mole crickets, so by spraying pesticides, you may inadvertently increase your mole cricket population by killing their enemies.

Method 3: Deep, infrequent watering encourages deep rooting, which increases the tolerance of the lawn to mole crickets and other root pests. High mowing of bahiagrass and St. Augustinegrass hides mole cricket damage and encourages deep rooting.

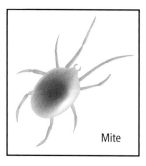

Mite

Mites

Mites are small spider relatives that feed on plants. Some mites, like the bermudagrass mite, are too small to see with the naked eye. The winter grain mite, which attacks bluegrass, bentgrass and the fine fescues, is small but its olive green body and eight red legs may be seen with the naked eye. The clover mite looks like rust-colored dust moving over the grass. Grasses become brown as mites suck out their juices. Control mites by spraying with insecticidal soap. Flowering plants in the Umbrel and Composite families support insects that feed on mites. Too much nitrogen fertilizer can exacerbate mite problems.

Scale Insects

Scale insects, also called "mealy bugs," are usually less than 1/16 in. across and may be covered with a cottony secretion, making them look like a fungus rather than an insect. Mainly a problem in California and the Gulf Coast states, they suck the juice out of grass near the crown, causing the grass to turn yellow and thin or even die out completely. "Ground pearls" are scales that attack roots. Dig up a grass plant and shake away the soil to see these. Control scale insects by drenching the lawn with insecticidal soap solution.

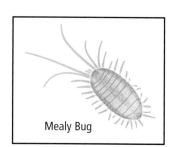

Mealy Bug

Greenbugs (aphids)

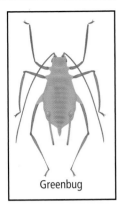

Greenbug

Greenbugs are small (1/16-in.) green or yellow bugs that seem to be made mostly out of the juices they suck out of plants. Wipe your hand over the grass and they will tumble off. They can be a problem on northern grasses in the shade, where damage shows up as pale areas with yellow streaking, but usually natural predators will control greenbugs. Flowering plants in the Umbrel and Composite families support insects that feed on aphids. They may also be killed with insecticidal soap. Too much nitrogen fertilizer invites greenbug problems, as does bluegrass forced to grow in the shade.

Fire ants

Fire ants include large, imported red and black species that are a problem in the Gulf States, Georgia, South Carolina and Arkansas. While they may benefit grass by aerating the soil and eating the larvae of pest insects, they detract from the beauty and utility of the lawn by building mounds and inflicting painful bites and stings. The ants cannot be completely eliminated, since new colonies will fly in to replace vanquished ones, but this effective "Two Step Method" of control is endorsed by Texas A&M University:

Step 1: Baiting. Spread fresh fire ant bait with a fertilizer spreader once or twice a year when the soil is not too dry, and temperatures are between 60 and 90°F. Baits will reduce the overall population of ants. The compromised colonies help prevent the invasion of new colonies with fertile queens. If you're unsure if old bait is rancid, put some by a hill when ants are feeding to see if it's taken.

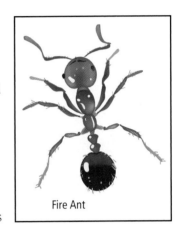

Fire Ant

Step 2: Treating Mounds. Wait a week or more after applying bait, then, if necessary, apply a contact pesticide directly to nuisance colonies in high-use areas. Apply when weather is not too hot and dry, since the queen will be higher in the mound and more vulnerable. Do not drench mounds in out-of–the-way areas, since these can help deter re-infestation of the high-use areas by new colonies. Contact insecticides for fire ants come as liquid drenches or as dusts and granules. Botanical contact insecticides that don't persist long in the environment include *d-limonene* (a citrus derivative), pyrethrins and rotenone.

Moles and Gophers

Moles eat worms and grubs, gophers eat the roots of plants, and both will damage a lawn. Moles leave ridges as they burrow just under the surface of the soil. They are about 6 in. long with gray or black fur and long pointed snouts. Gophers are bigger and burrow deeper, leaving crescent shaped piles of dirt on the surface. Most moles eat more earthworms than grubs, which is why eliminating grubs usually won't eliminate moles. Trapping is the most effective way to control both moles and gophers. Cats are also good at catching moles.

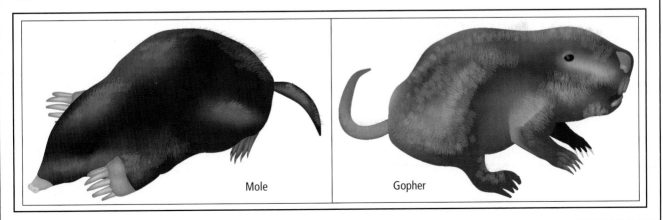

Mole   Gopher

Rust. Lawns infested with rust should be kept growing with adequate water and fertilization. Mow frequently, bagging and discarding clippings diligently.

Lawn Disease

Diseases of grass are almost all caused by fungi. Even more than insects and weeds, fungi require conditions to be just right. Golf course managers create those conditions by fertilizing, mowing and watering frequently, which is why many managers regularly spread fungicides against fungal diseases. The use of herbicides and insecticides also makes grass susceptible to disease by reducing populations of soil organisms that compete with or consume the fungi. The practices below reduce the vulnerability of your lawn to fungal disease.

1. Water deeply and infrequently. Water early in the morning, since night watering leaves grass blades wet. Fungi require a certain minimum length of time when the leaves are wet to establish.

2. Fertilize occasionally with compost or a slow-release fertilizer, but do not over-fertilize. Too much nitrogen increases the susceptibility of grass to disease. Undernourished grass is susceptible to disease as well.

3. Top-dress yearly with ¼ to ½ in. of compost or activated sewage sludge. Aerobically decomposed organic matter fertilizes the grass, while reducing the incidence and severity of turf diseases. This documented effect may be due to increased activity of soil organisms that feed on fungi and their spores.

4. Aerate, and dethatch yearly. This increases the vigor of the grass and permits air to circulate and dry out areas that would otherwise remain moist and anaerobic.

5. Mow to the correct height for the species, specifically avoid scalping your lawn. Use a sharp blade. Bag and discard clippings if infected with fungi.

6. Take a soil test and act on the recommendations. Soil outside the normal pH range is prone to fungal disease. Deficiencies of nutrients can make grass more susceptible to disease. NOTE: The over-application of one element can lead to deficiencies of other elements by displacement, which is another reason soil testing is important.

Common Grass Diseases

NOTE: The following discussion contains information on chemical controls of specific disease fungi. These fungicides should be used cautiously and as a last resort, after fully reading safety and environmental information.

Brown Patch/ Rhizoctonia Blight

Hits hardest when temperatures are in the low 80s and humidity is high, making it common in spring and fall in the South and in the summer in the North. High available nitrogen and a thick thatch layer favor the disease. Brown patch manifests as large spreading patches that start out as wilting grass and turn brown. Recovering grass in the middle may turn the patches into donut shapes. To control, use only slow-release fertilizers and avoid excessive nitrogen fertilization. Irrigate deeply when needed and in the morning only. Avoid traffic on affected areas. Mow affected areas last and collect the clippings. Spray with *Iprodione*, thiram or triadimefon. Resistant tall fescue *(Rebel II, Wrangler)* and perennial ryegrass *(Manhattan II, Pennant)* varieties are available.

Dollar Spot

Dollar spot usually appears as small spots (2 to 4 in. wide) on the lawn (See photo, next page) that may later grow together. The spots eventually dry and bleach to a pale brown. In the morning, you may see fluffy strands of the mycelium. This disease usually hits between 60 and 80°, under low nitrogen and potassium conditions. Fog, dew, or light irrigation may start the disease, even if the soil is dry. Water deeply when needed early in the morning and apply a light dose of fertilizer high in nitrogen. Sewage sludge (like *Milorganite*) works better than chemical sources of fertilizer according to university research. Mow high and frequently and remove the clippings. Dethatch if needed. Spray with *Iprodione* or thiram. Resistant varieties of fine fescues *(Biljart, Scaldis)*, perennial ryegrass *(Manhattan II)*, and Kentucky bluegrass *(Adelphi, Midnight)* are available.

Powdery Mildew

Appears as light patches of gray or white during cool damp weather in early summer to fall. Powdery mildew attacks Kentucky bluegrass, zoysiagrass and bermudagrass, especially when over-fertilized with nitrogen. Shade, temperatures between 60 and 70°F, and high humidity favor its growth. Avoid over-watering and over-fertilizing. Spray with *Iprodione* or triadimefon. Resistant varieties of Kentucky bluegrass *(America, Chateau)* and red fescue *(Cindy, Flyer)* are available.

Red Thread

Starts out as water-soaked spots, like other diseases, but this fungus eventually forms red threads of mycelium between the grass blades. Red thread hits cool-season grasses in the spring and fall when temperatures are between 68 and 75° and humidity is high. Spray with triadimefon. Resistant varieties of Kentucky bluegrass *(Chateau)*, perennial ryegrass *(Pennant)* and the fine fescues *(Biljart, Claudia)* are available.

Rust

Causes most damage to Kentucky bluegrass in summer and fall. Leaves will develop spots of rust-colored spores (See photo, previous page). Develops under moderately warm, humid conditions. Keep grass growing with morning watering and adequate fertilization, and mow frequently to remove spore spots. Spray with triadimefon. Resistant varieties include *America* and *Eclipse* Kentucky bluegrass and *Manhattan II* perennial ryegrass.

Stripe Smut

Susceptible varieties of bentgrass and Kentucky bluegrass will appear pale and stunted in the cool weather of spring and fall, developing stripes that start light and turn to black spore masses along the blades. Blades or the ends of blades die and become shredded as the disease advances. Dethatch and avoid over-watering and over-fertilizing to control stripe smut. Hot and dry weather will slow or even eliminate the disease. Resistant Kentucky bluegrass varieties include *America, Eclipse* and *Midnight.*

Pythium Blight

Mostly affects cool-season grasses in hot, moist weather. It requires fourteen hours of rain, fog, or high humidity to get going. Small spots appear slimy and water soaked at first, then infected blades turn light brown. Smaller spots converge into larger blighted areas eventually. The white cotton of the mycelium may be visible on top of infected patches in the early morning. Water deeply and infrequently and avoid watering in the evening. Avoid walking on turf when

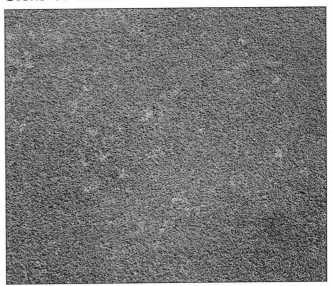

Dollar spot. Deep, infrequent morning irrigation, high mowing, and adequate slow-release nitrogen help control dollar spot.

Necrotic ring is a common disease of newly sodded bluegrass lawns. Water and fertilize adequately to keep infected grass alive.

wet. Reduce frequency of mowing. Spray *Ethazole* or *Chloroneb. Amigo* tall fescue is resistant to the disease.

Necrotic Ring Spot

Attacks Kentucky bluegrass and to a lesser extent bentgrass and fine fescue. Starts in spring but causes rings of dead grass to appear in summer (See photo above). Rings may be green in the center. Keep grass properly watered, mowed and fertilized, with more frequent, morning watering needed to keep infected grass alive. Aerate if needed. Spray fenarimol or *Iprodione.*

Raking is part and parcel of just about any lawn renovation or repair project. If you haven't done it already, invest in some high-quality rakes—See page 13.

disease and frost damage or just plain kill your grass outright.

Repairing the lawn

Fortunately, planting, leveling, aerating and dethatching doesn't always need to happen on a grand scale. Often a lawn will be great except for those spots where the dog urinated or the gas spilled or that buried tree trunk rotted away. Dealing with these small-scale ills is not different in principal than correcting large-scale problems, but you don't need all the expensive rental tools, and you don't need to call in a lot of IOUs for help. Below we cover leveling and planting small areas.

Core aerating

Power core aerators require some physical strength and practice to control. Practice using them away from obstacles.

Use a core aerator once or twice yearly on compacted clay soils or soils with thatch problems. If you overseed a southern lawn in the fall, and it needs aerating, you might as well kill two birds with one stone and aerate before

Aerating tips:

- Consider hiring a lawn service to perform this strenuous task.
- Don't rent a solid-spike aerator.
- Haul the machine home in a trailer, truck or van when empty of water.
- Practice aerating on an open area of your lawn.
- Go up and down, not across slopes.
- Raise tines when approaching stone or cement.
- Fertilize and seed after aerating, if desired.

Renovating & Repairing

A tired lawn with thin grass, bare patches and/or a thick layer of thatch can be revived with rental tools. A power core aerator lets air and water into compacted soil and speeds the decomposition of the thatch layer. A power rake tears out thatch and scratches the soil to let the roots and stems breathe and allows wet havens of disease and insects to dry out. Both tools expose soil so new seed may be planted (See page 21).

These tools can be used in conjunction with herbicides to completely replace a sick, weedy lawn without tilling or exposing the soil to erosion. Power raking is harder on grass and should generally be done at the beginning of the peak of the growing season, when the lawns will have the ability and time to recover—September for cool-season grasses and May or June for warm-season grasses. Power raking at other times can invite weeds, preparing to overseed, as this will help the winter grass establish. Seeds that fall into the holes grow well since they are protected from drying. Aerating before fertilizing, adding lime or adding sulfur helps these amendments penetrate. Avoid aerating in hot, dry weather since the holes can dry out the soil, and avoid aerating when weeds like dandelions are in seed, since the weeds will root in the holes.

How to aerate

Water a dry, hard lawn thoroughly a couple of days before aerating to soften the soil. Rent a heavy aerator with hollow tines that pull plugs of soil from your lawn. Solid-tine aerators are not as good. Often, aerators have a place to put water to make them heavier. Don't try to transport them full of water, but do fill them before using them. Ask the rental center to demonstrate how to use the machine and, if needed, how to adjust any weights for use on hills. At home, flag obstacles like sprinkler heads and shallow pipes or wires. Set the tines at maximum depth and begin aerating an open

AERATING

Aerate to let oxygen, water, nutrients, and even grass seed into compacted, heavy, or thatchy soil. You may also aerate before amending soil or before overseeding grass seed. Don't aerate a hot, dry lawn, and don't aerate when lots of weeds are in seed.

part of your lawn. Aerate once in a parallel line pattern, then again perpendicular to the first pattern. Ultimately, you want holes every 2 or 3 in. Leave the soil plugs on the surface; they will help break down the thatch layer. If you want to get

rid of the plugs more quickly, you may break the plugs up with the back of a rake or by dragging a piece of chain link fencing over the lawn. This may work better after the plugs have dried out.

Manual aerators. For a small lawn, a foot-driven aerator like the one shown here works well. A garden fork pushed in all the way and rocked back and forth works okay too, except no plugs are pulled.

Dethatching rakes are handy for smaller areas, but for most folks they're too labor-intensive for use dethatching an entire yard.

Dethatching

Thatch is the buildup of dead plant matter that collects around the crowns of grass plants in a yard. By itself it isn't harmful, but it does make an excellent home for pests and fungi, and can prevent nutrients from reaching the living plant roots if it gets extremely heavy. The process of getting rid of thatch, called *dethatching,* can be done either with a heavy, sharp-tined dethatching rake or a rented power dethatcher.

Bermudagrass, bluegrass and zoysiagrass are good candidates for power raking, since they build up thatch and become choked, but other grasses can also develop the problem. A layer of thatch more than ½ in. thick is considered too much, and even small amounts of thatch buildup should be removed if you want to overseed your lawn.

Power raking will damage the grass in the short run. With warm-season grasses, power rake in late spring or early summer. With cool-season grasses, August or September is best. If you are power raking to overseed winter grass on a southern lawn, then do so in October or November, but not as aggressively as you would in the spring.

Rent a verticutter for thick thatch, especially on tough southern grasses, or if you are replanting a lawn and are not too concerned about damaging the existing grass. Rent a power rake for cool-season lawn maintenance.

What is thatch?

Thatch is a soft, spongy layer between the soil and the grass blades made up of roots, stems, and runners. It is not caused by leaving clippings on the lawn. You can't see thatch unless you dig a wedge out of your lawn, and then look for a peaty layer between the soil and where the grass emerges. Less than ½ in. of thatch is not a problem, and can actually protect the lawn against drying and frost damage. More than ½ in. can lead to an uneven, unmanageable lawn susceptible to lawn mower scalping, drought, cold, heat stress, and insects. Simply speaking, water, nutrients and the grass roots stay matted in the thatch layer instead of moving down into the soil where temperature and moisture levels are more constant. Zoysiagrass, bluegrass, and bermudagrass are all highly susceptible to thatch formation.

Causes of Thatch:
- Frequent, shallow watering
- Too much nitrogen fertilizer
- Infrequent mowing
- Overuse of pesticides

HOW TO DETHATCH BY POWER RAKING

Set the tine depth. Lower the tines of a power rake to the pavement to adjust the depth the flails will penetrate.

Aggressive power raking will damage grass, and should be done prior to optimal growing conditions—early September for cool-season northern grasses and late spring for warm-season southern grasses. Exposure of dirt makes seeding possible.

DETHATCHING OPTIONS: POWER RAKE TINES VS. SLIT SEEDER (VERTICUTTER) BLADES

Power rakes. Flexible flails are used on power rakes. These are more popular on the softer, less thatchy, cool-season grasses of the North.

Slit seeders and verticutters use moving blades for a more aggressive cut. These are used for dethatching purposes on tough, southern grasses and for direct seeding everywhere.

Slit seeders are verticutters fitted with a hopper that accepts seed then injects it into the slits as it cuts. Load the hopper with seed and set it for the recommended spread rate for the species of grass you're planting (See pages 36 to 46).

Set the cutters so they rip into the ground about ¼ in. deep, then make parallel passes across the area to be overseeded. Keep an eye on the hopper to make sure you don't run out of seed.

Overseeding

Thin or damaged lawns often can be improved simply by doing some minor preparation, then adding fresh grass seed—called "overseeding." Exclusive of any soil amendments that may be needed, the primary preparation involves getting rid of thatch and roughening or scarifying the soil so the seed has somewhere safe to settle.

For overseeding an entire lawn, there's no better tool than a slit seeder or a verticutter. The first order of business is to set the cutters so they rip into the ground to the correct depth for seeding. To set the cutters, first put the machine on a hard surface. For a living lawn, set the blades to cut ⅛ to ¼ in. into the soil. You may go deeper on a lawn that's been killed with herbicides and will be completely reseeded. First, zero the blades by seeing where they just touch the pavement, and then add the necessary depth using the gauge as a guide.

Overseeding with a verticutter or a slit seeder

Using a verticutter. First mow the lawn as low as possible with your lawn mower. This low mowing is critical if you intend to seed. Run the machine over the yard in a parallel-line pattern. If you don't have a bagger, rake up the lawn after this first pass. If more dethatching is needed, run perpendicular to the first pattern and rake again. If you will be seeding, you must expose dirt between existing grass plants. For a very dense thatch, you might need to tackle dethatching over two sessions spaced months apart.

Using a slit seeder. If you will be planting with a slit seeder, less preparation is needed since the seed is injected into a furrow cut by the machine. You should still address a serious thatch problem prior to planting. You may compost the thatch if you maintain a hot pile; otherwise, throw out thatch that is infested with stolons and rhizomes from aggressive warm-season grasses that could become weeds in your garden.

Planting Bare Spots

For best results, repair bare spots in the late spring and early summer for warm-season grasses and in the early fall (preferable) or early spring for the cool-season grasses. This will save you the headache of trying to keep new grass alive when the weather and weeds are not in your favor.

Clear a bare spot of all weeds and straggling grass right out to where the grass is thick and healthy. If needed, correct problems that led to grass's decline. This may mean adjusting the spray patterns on a sprinkler system, removing a rock or other object from under the damaged area, or removing oil- or chemical-saturated soil and replacing it with fresh.

Prepare the ground as you would for a full lawn. Cover ground planted with sprigs or plugs with a thin layer of straw, compost or peat to keep the soil moist. If you use seed, you will either need to rake the seed and soil lightly until most of the seeds are covered, then cover it with a thin layer of straw; or, cover seed with ¼ in. of compost or peat without raking. Water the area thoroughly. Water only intermittently if runoff is a problem, particularly with seed, which is easily dislodged. Then, keep the area from drying out until the grass emerges, watering gradually more deeply and less frequently after that. Keep sprigged or plugged areas weeded.

1 Remove any weed roots, then incorporate compost or peat moss and starter fertilizer into the soil using a fork or shovel. Smooth the ground with a garden rake, tamp it down with a shovel, a roller, a hand tamper```` or your feet. Smooth again.

2 When the soil is graded and tamped correctly, your feet will sink in no more that ½ in. If you will plant sod, the grade needs to be a little lower than the surrounding grass. Rough-up tamped soil with a rake, then plant seeds, sprigs or plugs.

3 Top-dress the unraked, broadcast seed—peatmoss is used above. Rake in seed that will be covered only with straw to provide better soil contact. Grass seed should never be buried more than ¼ in. Finally, lightly tamp down or roll planted area.

Leveling a Lawn

Roll a lumpy lawn in the spring with a partly-filled lawn roller when the soil is soft but not muddy. Alternatively, top-dress with ½ in. of topsoil once or twice a year until the lawn becomes smooth. The latter method improves the health of the grass too.

For large dips and humps, such as those that occur when a buried stump rots away, you will need to regrade the soil below the sod. Water the problem area the day before working on it. This will make the soil soft but not muddy, and the grass resilient to the stress of transplanting. Use a square-nose spade to chop off the roots attaching the sod to the ground as you peel, rolling the sod as you go. Work-in compost and a little high-phosphorous fertilizer (if allowed in your area) before leveling, raking

Top-dress uneven lawns with ½ in. of topsoil once or twice a year. This helps keep the lawn level and also improves the health and drought resiliency of the grass.

HOW TO RAISE DIPS IN THE LAWN

1 Cut a large "X" over the dip or hump. Peel back the triangles of sod from the center of the "X," leaving 1 to 2 in. of thickness to the mat of roots and dirt.

2 Remove or add soil as needed to level the area, accounting for the thickness of the sod itself. Also mix fertilizer and compost into the final substrate. Rake, tamp, and rake again.

and tamping the soil. Tamp down worked-up soil with a hand tamper, lawn roller or improvised tamping tool. Don't pack it so tight that the roots can't penetrate it to establish themselves. Give the area a final light raking to leave the soil flat, but a little rough, to receive the sod's roots. Replace the sod, roll or tamp lightly, and fill in the seams between the pieces with compost or topsoil. Water the repair deeply, and then water it daily until the sod re-roots. Add soil or compost a little at a time to the top of the sod as a fine-tuning leveling agent.

Underwater edges

Paved surfaces that drop below the level of the lawn may end up puddled and muddy every time it rains. Ideally, surfaces should drain onto the lawn, not vice versa. Remove soil from beneath sod to bring down the level of the lawn below adjoining paved surfaces.

1 To lower a lawn area next to pavement, first peel back the sod in the lower area with a flat-edge spade or a rented sod kicker (a better tool choice).

2 Remove plenty of soil, then work compost and and fertilizer into what remains. Rake, tamp or roll, and re-rake.

3 Tamp the dirt slightly, then roughen the surface of the soil with a rake. Roll the sod back and tamp it down. Keep the sod well watered until it re-roots.

3 The final edge of the sod, when laid back down, should drop slightly below the level of the adjoining pavement.

Accent Plantings & Border Treatments

Border treatments define your yard by creating shapes, adding colors and texture, and even introducing entirely new functions. If you want a lawn with relaxed curving edges, for example, you can achieve it by building border beds to establish those curves. For a quiet, shady spot to kick back with the newspaper, carefully selected, strategically planted trees, shrubs and perennials hold the key by providing shade and muffling noise—something that the grass lawn just can't do by itself.

In this section, we'll look at some fundamentals of creating and maintaining your lawn accent plantings—including the planning of non-grass areas; the establishment of edged beds; the planting and care of annuals and perennials, trees and shrubs, and groundcovers; and the use of mulches.

Planning & Design

In "An Exercise in Practical Imagination" on pages 6 to 9, we suggest a strategy for planning your yard so it will look and function as you'd like. Please take the time to review this section as you consider ways to embellish your yard with accent and border plantings in planting beds.

To begin, you need to be able to answer the following questions:

1) How much sunlight does the area get? Half a day of direct sun or a full day of dappled sun is usually enough for sun-loving and partial-sun-requiring plants. If your yard area doesn't get these minimum amounts of sun, you'll have to limit your plant selections to shade and part-shade plants. Keep in mind, though, that while many shade plants can tolerate some morning sun, they may dry and burn in hot afternoon sun. So just as you shouldn't plant sun-loving plants in deep shade, neither should you plant shade plants in areas that receive more than a half-day of sunlight. Remember also that the north sides of buildings cast a longer shadow as summer progresses.

2) Are your growing seasons dry and will you irrigate regularly? Good garden centers and plant tags provide information on the moisture requirements of plants.

3) How tall and wide do the plant varieties you are considering become? Ignore the current size of plant material you are buying; rather, situate plant material with an eye to how it will look when it reaches its full size. Space plants according to recommendations on tags.

Once you've made these preliminary assessments, map out your planting beds on graph paper, paying close attention to make sure the dimensions and symbols are to scale. In the illustration below, we used a scale of one square equals one square foot. An accurate rendering such as this allows you to plan the bed completely before making any plant purchases or turn-

Design tips for accent planting

Know your square footage and light. Measure and record the spaces you're buying plants for, and note the light zone of each: sun, part-sun, shade or deep shade.

Work from back to front. When planting border beds, keep tall plants to the back and move forward with progressively smaller plants. Shrubs work well against the foundations of houses; short annuals and perennials make colorful accents in the foreground of a bed.

Be conscious of scale. Little plants at the nursery can get very big with time. Small yards need smaller beds, trees and shrubs. Big spaces need big trees and shrubs and/or wide masses of annuals or perennials.

Keep it simple, repeat masses. Too many different plants lead to chaos. Select a few species that work together, then plant each species in masses of three, five, seven or more (odd numbers work better). Repeat these masses to unify the landscape.

ing any dirt. Armed with a good plan, you'll know exactly how many plants of each species you need. Use information from your local garden center catalogs to select plants that will work with the size, the zone and the light conditions of your planting area.

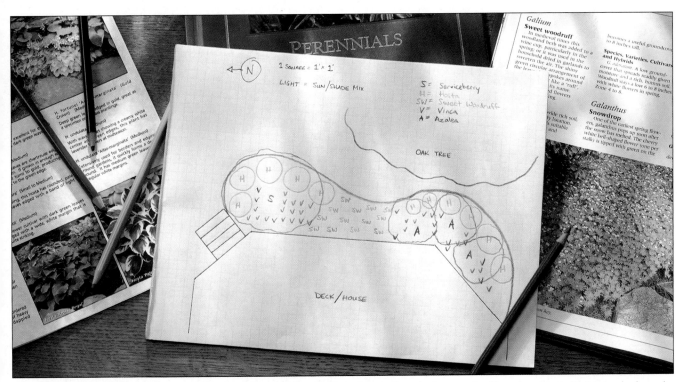

The plan shown above uses a one-foot-per-square scale. Each plant is allowed approximately the room it will require at maturity. Larger shrubs and trees may share space with smaller, shade-tolerant plants. You may even plant sun-loving varieties near young trees and shrubs that will take years to overgrow these underplantings.

Ornamentals: The meanings of the terms

Annuals: Ornamental annuals, by definition, die after one growing season. They are planted for intense, prolonged periods of bloom or showy foliage. A number of "annuals," such as the red *Pelargonium* geraniums in the photo above, are actually tender perennials that are grown in areas where they're killed by winter cold.

Perennials: Perennials die down to the ground after the growing season in temperate climates and, under favorable growing conditions, regrow from surviving underground parts. In the photo to the right, sweet woodruff (flowering), hostas (big, variegated leaves), and *Epimedium* (upper right of photo) complement one another in a shade garden.

PERENNIALS

Woody Plants: Shrubs, trees, and woody vines all have above-ground parts that do not die back and can survive periods of dormancy. This characteristic allows woody plants to get bigger every year, sometimes for many years. Spring-flowering trees (like the ornamental pears pictured to the right) use sugars stored from the previous year to put out early, stunning floral displays.

Groundcovers: Groundcovers are perennial or woody plants used in masses to form a mat of a single species over the ground. Most plants used as groundcovers may also be used individually or in smaller numbers in mixed planting beds; hence, "groundcover" describes a particular plant only when it is used in masses. *Pachysandra,* the groundcover featured below, thrives in moist, acid soils beneath trees.

NOTE: Contrary to a popular misconception, "groundcover" does not refer only to very low plants, such as Creeping Charlie, that have the general look and feel of a lawn and can even withstand light foot traffic.

WOODY PLANTS

GROUNDCOVERS

Preparing a Planting Bed

Plan to plant perennials, shrubs or trees in the spring, late summer, or early fall, when at least a month of mild temperatures (neither hot nor freezing) follows. Use your scale plan drawing as a reference for laying out the planting area. Ground-marking paint, a hose or a rope can be used to outline the area.

First, turn the soil with a garden fork to ten inches deep. Amend the forked soil with a three-inch layer of compost, composted manure, peat or other organic material (See "Estimating Quantities," page 56, for calculating volumes of materials in cubic yards). Add a complete fertilizer, following the label directions for application and coverage. If you are incorporating quantities of un-decomposed organic matter, like leaves or sawdust, add extra fertilizer to help the material decompose without robbing the plants of nitrogen. A soil test can alert you to the need for micronutrients, sulfur or lime (see page 49), but it's best not to use these unless you're positive they're needed—they can harm plants if added indiscriminately. Rototill to mix the soil, compost and amendments.

If you are using a sod kicker on grass, cut just inside your bed line with the kicker to establish the border. Next, slice along your bed border with a flat-nosed gar-den spade, cutting a vertical edge eight to ten inches deep. Toss the dirt to the middle or back of your bed and remove the sod chunks and weeds. Your edge may seem deep, but you'll lose most of this height after grading the bed later. Dig an edge trench along pavement as well to make grading easier. Once the dirt is removed in this manner, lay any edging material you intend to use around the perimeter of the planting bed.

Next, shape the soft, turned soil of the planting bed with the back of a garden rake. Avoid creating steep slopes near the edges of the bed, as steep slopes are more prone to erosion of soil and loss of any mulch or loose topping. It's best to start the slope at the back of the bed and distribute the drop-off as evenly as possible across the bed. In the process of grading, the level of the amended soil in the planting bed area may approach or even surpass the surrounding lawn area. If you find this is happening, don't compact the soil, remove it. Ideally, the surface of the soil in the graded bed should be two to four inches below ground level. If you'll be adding mulch, you'll need three or four inches of lip at lawn and pavement edges to keep the mulch from washing out of the bed—generally, landscape edging is installed to provide the lip. For an un-mulched bed, leave an open border of an inch or two at pavement edges and three inches next to lawns to keep the grass from growing into the bed.

CLEARING THE PLANTING AREA

Kill vegetation in the planting area. Water a day or two in advance of spraying vegetation with glyphosate (Roundup, Kleenup, GLYPHOS). Repeat procedure two weeks later for tough weeds and wait for herbicide to fully kill the plants. Roots and stumps of dead plants may be left in place if they do not interfere with planting. Dig up woody plants and large perennials that will grow back or interfere with planting. Use a spade, mattock and axe. Kill living stumps left in place with concentrated glyphosate painted on the fresh cut.

CAUTION: Does this scene look familiar? Using the old truck and a towing chain to pull out a stubborn stump or woody shrub is an idea that many of us have had at one time or another, and perhaps even attempted once. But not twice. Under the right conditions it can work, but more likely than not, you'll experience one or more of the following outcomes: damage to your vehicle or anything else that's in the path of the stump or trunk when it catapults out of the ground under force; deep furrows in your lawn created by spinning tires; damage from chain snapback if the object being pulled snaps. In short, it's very dangerous. You're much better off using saws and shovels for the extraction.

Excavating & Preparing the Soil

Peel out sod in the planting area. Simplify the job by renting a sod kicker (shown here) from a garden center or hardware store. If you've used an herbicide to kill the grass, the sod may be tilled under instead of removed. If your planting bed is on a steep slope, it is sometimes necessary to forego proper bed preparation and plant directly into sod that's been killed with herbicide. The roots system of the dead sod holds the soil in place.

TIP: If you're careful removing the sod, you can often re-lay it in another part of the yard. Or, you can re-use it by composting it. Turn the sod upside down and layer it into a compost pile that's dish-shaped on top to collect water. In a year, the compost from the sod may be sifted and used as a lawn topdressing.

Clear out debris. Buried building debris, old pavers, edgings, gravel, cypress mulches, plastic sheeting, large rocks and all other debris that could potentially interfere with the growth of your new plants must be removed and disposed of before preparing and amending the soil for a new planting bed.

Amend soil with specific fertilizer elements and lime or sulfur, according to the results of a soil test. Fork and then till in 3 or 4 in. of organic matter. Even if no soil test is done, a balanced fertilizer may also be tilled in at this time. A rototiller will make quick work of the soil blending and turning task.

Edging

A well-defined edge is necessary for a planting bed to look neat and "intentional." Without one, the plants will sprawl out into the lawn, the lawn grass will migrate into the bed, and the effectiveness of the planting bed will be reduced. In most cases, edging is used to define the border. It may be just the raw, spade-cut side of the sod, or it can be any of a number of edging materials.

Edging is not needed if the planting bed abuts a paved surface. If material from the planting bed does wash onto the paved surface, you'll need to excavate material from the planting bed to lower its surface.

Edging Options

• **The Spade Edge.** Many gardeners prefer to take a laid-back approach to edging, simply relying on the sharp edges of the cut sod to create a border for their planting bed. This method does have some advantages that make it worth considering. It's very easy to make; just cut the sod off vertically at the side of the lawn, leaving a short "cliff." Rhizomes that grow out of this edge will be discouraged when they encounter only air, although some will certainly find their way into the bed. The impermanence of the spade edge is something you may find desirable; there will be nothing to dig up if you decide to move the boundary of the bed.

A spade-cut edge will need to be recut at least once a year to keep creeping grasses (or creeping garden plants) in check.

• **Plastic Band Edging.** Easily the most common edging product, plastic band edging (also called landscaper's edging) is inexpensive and easy to install on straight or curved beds. It helps keep grasses that spread by rhizomes, like bluegrass and bermudagrass, from spreading into beds. Don't try to use plastic edging to contain raised beds or to keep mulch off a path—they are too flexible for above ground use. If you live in the North, get plastic edges that are staked in place to resist frost heave. You'll find quite a range of qualities in plastic edging. The more expensive plastic edging is thicker and more rigid, which makes it easier to install and longer lasting.

• **Brick Edging.** In addition to contributing attractive color and new texture to your yard, brick edging provides a mowing strip so you can mow right up to the edge of the grass. You can use just about any kind of brick product to make edging. Concrete landscaping pavers tend to be the most durable, and you'll find them in many sizes, colors and shapes that offer a number of layout options. But ordinary building bricks will work just fine, too. If you have any leftover or reclaimed bricks lying around, put them to work as edging, and feel free to mix and match as you please.

THE SPADE EDGE

Slice the sod. After outlining the planting bed, use a spade (a flat spade works best) to make deep, perpendicular slices all around the border. Remove all weeds and plants to create a gap between the cut edge and the border plants. Avoid stepping on the sod too close to the border area.

Create a buffer zone. A band of mulch between grass and bed plants enhances the border effect and suppresses migration. The mulch should be just below ground level. In the photo above, cypress mulch is used, mostly because of its ability to mat and resist spill-over into the lawn. Avoid stone mulches—they'll mix with the soil and never decompose.

PLASTIC BAND EDGING

Use plenty of stakes. The spade-cut edge can be made impervious to aggressive grass rhizomes with plastic edging. The tubular crown of the edging should be set so half of the crown is below ground level to keep the edging clear of lawn mower blades. Generous use of metal edging stakes helps keep the edging safe from movement caused by ground forces, including frost heave. Make sure to use the correct connectors to join the mating ends of edging strips (higher quality plastic edging comes in shorter rolls that require more joints).

Backfill with soil. Using an inverted garden rake, rake the soil in the planting bed right up to the edging. The pressure of the soil against it helps keep the edging stationary. Move or remove soil as needed to provide room for mulch or other topdressing materials.

BRICK EDGING

Prepare a base for the bricks. Dig a trench for bricks or pavers. The trench should be about ½ in. deeper than the thickness of your bricks. Bury a strip of landscape fabric at the bottom of the trench, then cover the strip with a ½ to 1-in.-thick layer of coarse sand. Lay the bricks or pavers onto the sand base. The top of each brick should be at or slightly above ground level to create a mowing strip. Press down on each brick to set it into the base.

Fill in with soil. Cut back any overhanging landscape fabric that will be visible, then backfill up to the bricks so the soil covers roughly half the thickness. Backfill with soil between the bricks and the lawn, as well.

Mulch

Mulch is any material that covers the ground between plants. Mulch keeps the ground moist and suppresses the new growth of weeds. Loose mulches let air and water through. Perennial weeds that already have roots can usually push through loose mulch. Organic loose mulches, like shredded and chipped wood products, improve the soil as they rot. Barrier mulches and products suppress growth of all weeds, not just seedlings, but plastic and fabric barrier mulches prevent organic mulches on top from adding organic matter to the soil. Barrier mulches need to be covered with loose mulch to keep them from degrading in the sun or blowing away. Thick mulches used only during the winter protect tender plants from winterkill.

Typical Loose Mulches

Chipped mulches. Bark and wood chips look nice, but do not hold together well on slopes or in other areas where they are not easily contained. Chips generally last longer than shredded products. Do not turn cypress chips into the soil—they decompose very slowly and cause drainage problems. If you are renovating a bed, remove chipped mulch first, work the soil, then replace the mulch with fresh product.

Shredded mulches. Shredded bark and wood hold together better on slopes than chips, they can be purchased in bulk (as opposed to bagged), and they look good. Mulches like the shredded cypress bark shown here are expensive, though, and need to be replenished yearly.

Chipped mulches decompose slowly but do not stick together well.

Shredded mulches hold to slopes better. They rot more quickly than chipped mulches.

Shredder/chipper wastes are often free, and have a higher nutrient content than most commercial mulches.

Cocoa mulch is expensive, but is darker and more refined than some of the other organic mulches.

Stone mulches are low maintenance at first, but they can burn plants in hot sun and eventually become contaminated with dirt and debris.

Winter mulches completely cover cut back perennials. They prevent thawing and re-freezing and winter drying of tender plants.

Landscape fabric lets water and air through but keeps weeds down. Use under mineral mulches.

Newspaper blocks grass and other perennial weeds and then rots away after these weeds die.

Black plastic is not good for plants but may be needed near buildings to keep water away from the foundation.

Shredder/Chipper Wastes

Municipalities and yard waste collection facilities often give shredder/chipper wastes away free or for a very low cost. They are the ground-up remains of branches, leaves and logs. These mulches vary in quality, but after a month or so exposed to the elements, it becomes more difficult to distinguish shredder/chipper wastes from more expensive, commercial shredded mulches.

Organic byproducts. Marsh hay, cocoa shells, buckwheat hulls, partially composted farm animal bedding, and other byproducts of agriculture and forestry make fine mulches. Avoid products that may contain weed seeds, such as hay.

Mineral mulches. Stone mulches laid on landscape fabric create a distinct design effect, but do have some disadvantages. Vegetation that falls on the mulch eventually rots and, along with dust and dirt, forms a layer of compost within the mulch that supports weeds. Removal and replacement of a stone mulch that has bonded with dirt and compost is difficult. Reserve mineral mulches for accessible, cleanable areas with few plants.

Winterizing mulches. These are thick, fluffy mulches applied to newly planted areas or to plants that may be susceptible to winterkill. Winter mulches include straw, leaves and pine branches, which are applied six to 12 inches thick after the ground freezes or is close to freezing. They are left in place until spring.

Weed Barriers

Newspapers and cardboard. When layered on the soil or sod around plants, wet newspapers or cardboard present a temporary barrier to tough perennial weeds. Use newspapers with predominantly black ink. Cover newspaper and cardboard with soil or another mulch to hold it in place. The paper, cardboard and mulch will rot in place, improving the soil structure after suppressing weeds.

Landscaping fabric. Used mostly in exterior construction projects, such as installing patios, landscape fabric can be installed under rock mulches to prevent perennial weeds from sprouting. It does allow water and air to get through, so it may be used around plants. Though landscaping fabric is permanent, weeds eventually colonize the compost and dirt that settles on top of the fabric. When covered with loose organic mulches, fabric will prevent those organic materials from improving the soil beneath.

Black plastic. Not considered appropriate for gardening purposes by most professionals, black plastic is often used as a weed barrier by homeowners. Unlike landscape fabric, it does not permit air and water to get through, and it will degrade more rapidly than you might think, creating a mess that deteriorates the general condition of the soil.

Tips for applying mulch:

• Fine, dense mulches should be spread in 1-in.-thick layers; medium-density mulches, like shredded bark, should be spread two or three inches thick; very airy mulches, like salt marsh hay, need to be spread at least 6 in. deep; winter mulches must be at least 6 to 12 in. thick to be successful insulators.

• Do not pile mulches (except winter mulches) right up against plants unless you know that the plant tolerates close mulching. Instead, form basins or "donuts" around plants with the mulch.

• Avoid applying mulch to slopes. A mulch may be temporarily held to a slope with coarse netting and stakes, however, until a permanent groundcover takes over.

Experiment with layouts while the plants are still in their containers. Allow the recommended distance between plants, since the plants will get much bigger—although it may take perennials two or three growing seasons, or even longer, to fill in completely.

Adding Plants to a New Planting Bed

Once your soil is amended and tilled you are ready to plant. With small plants that come in cell trays or pots, you may wish to lay the mulch before planting. For larger potted plants, plant before mulching. Either way, lay out the plants, while still in their containers, prior to planting. The goal is to find a natural-looking arrangement that allows each plant its approximate recommended space. Experiment a bit until you find a layout that pleases you.

NOTE: The information in this section presumes that you are planting in a new planting bed that has been prepared and amended according to the information on the previous pages. For stand-alone accent plants, prepare the planting area as if it were a tiny planting bed, according to the information on pages 128 to 133.

How to plant your plants

Remove plants from the pots, unless the pots are made of peat. Break roots free with your hands, or use a knife if the roots are growing in a tight circle. Take care to keep the root system or ball intact. You may plant in a slight depression to facilitate watering, but the soil should not run over the stem, as this can cause rot. Dig the hole a bit shallow if you will be laying thick mulch that would otherwise run high on the stem. The majority of the pot ball of even small cell-tray plants needs to be embedded in dirt, however.

Do not force the plant into a hole that's too small or too shallow. When the plant is in place, backfill around it with loose soil (don't pack it) then cover the area around the plant with two or three inches of mulch.

TIPS FOR PLANTING ACCENT & BORDER PLANTS

Provide irrigation. Lay soaker hoses or drip irrigation lines before you begin planting.

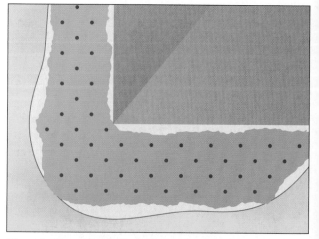

Plant single-species beds in intersecting diagonal rows. Plants are best spaced in roughly triangular patterns. This allows equidistant planting and prevents the "garden row" effect. When planting a single plant species as a groundcover, as in the illustration above, the plants may be set out in intersecting diagonal rows. Spacing of plants in mixed gardens varies with species and is looser and more natural.

HOW TO PLANT LARGE ACCENT PLANTS

1 Support the root ball with one hand while pulling off the pot. Make three vertical cuts in the root ball and peel out some roots if the root ball is tightly circled with roots (the hosta shown above does not require that roots be peeled free).

2 Plant annuals and perennials to the same depth they were growing in their container. Set the plant in the hole, positioned so it is perfectly upright. Fill in around it with soil, taking care not to cover up any part of the stem. Do not overpack the soil.

3 Larger plants are most easily mulched after planting. Keep the mulch thick between plants and thin near the stems. Heavy mulch piled against a plant stem can promote disease.

TIPS FOR PLANTING

Small plants. Lay mulch before planting small plants that come in cell trays, like many groundcovers and the annuals shown above. If the soil is soft, you may push aside the mulch and press the root ball into the soil with only a little digging. Again, you want the top of the root ball at about soil level, but with small plants you'll sometimes plant a little high so the plant stem is not buried too deeply in mulch.

Extricating stubborn plants. To remove a jammed plastic pot from the root ball, slice the pot in a couple of spots with a utility knife. Do not use the stem as a handle to try to get the plant out of the pot.

Tips for Planting on Slopes

Cut soil from up-slope to build a solid berm down-slope, creating a mini terrace that collects water for the plant.

• **Use the no-till method** of planting by spraying old vegetation with glyphosate herbicide and planting without turning the soil. As an alternative to broadcast fertilizing, put a little time-release balanced fertilizer in the bottom of each planting hole. This prevents fertilizer runoff.

• **If sloped ground is tilled,** it's useful to shape the soil into a series of ridges and troughs that run across the slope. These contour ridges keep water from running down the slope and creating erosion gullies. In the tillage process, you may incorporate organic matter and any amendments called for by a soil test, which is one reason to use this method instead of no-till. Make ridges by tilling across the slope or by forming the troughs and crests with a shovel.

DIVIDING OLD PLANTS:
Why & When to Do It

Most overgrown perennials may be divided to increase the size of flowers, improve the health of the plants, and as a cost-free way to acquire new plants for your yard. Divide fall-blooming plants in the spring, leaving time for the plants to establish before hot weather. Divide spring- and summer-flowering plants in late summer or early fall, at least six weeks before the ground freezes.

Tip: *Water dry ground well a day or more before dividing; the ground should be moist but not muddy when you divide the plants.*

HOW TO DIVIDE PLANTS

1 Cut the top foliage down to six inches, or by two-thirds, to reduce evaporation and to make working with the plants easier. Then, dig up the plants to be divided, preserving as much of the root system as is practical.

2 Plants with multiple stems may be pulled apart so that each new plant has three to five stems. Plants with thick, fleshy central crowns (like the hosta above) should be divided with a spade or knife so each section has some of the crown. Plants that grow by rhizome, such as irises, can be cut or broken apart. Each piece of rhizome should have a fan of leaves and some roots.

3 Discard any rotten or dead plant material and remove all weeds and weed roots. Keep the uprooted plants moist and plant at the same level they were growing at previously. Leave plenty of room for the new plants to grow to their full size, as crowding usually reduces flowering. Keep plants watered until established.

Remove spent flowers or flower stalks. This is called "deadheading." With many plants, deadheading encourages new blooms. With the hostas shown here, it simply neatens up the plants.

Topdress annually. A yearly topdressing of compost and fertilizer followed by a fresh layer of mulch supplies nutrients and valuable organic matter to your garden plants while keeping weeds down.

Caring for Plants, New & Old

Your new planting will need a little extra care at first. Importantly, you'll need to water as soon as the plants begin to wilt, possibly every day in hot weather. Gradually move to deep, infrequent watering as the roots establish. Most mature perennials prefer that the ground dries to a depth of 8 to 12 inches between waterings. If you have a zoned in-ground watering system (See page 82), set the controls so mulched perennial beds and groundcover zones receive less frequent watering than the lawn once the plants are established. But when you do water, water deeply.

Hand-pull weeds that push through the mulch. Deadhead to encourage flowering. Fertilize yearly with a slow-release balanced fertilizer for flowering plants. Alternatively or additionally, spread an inch or two of compost or composted manure on top of the old mulch yearly, and replenish the mulch on top of that.

Cut back perennials to two or three inches when they start to go dormant in the fall. Uproot annuals. Apply a layer of mulch around recently planted or winter-tender perennials.

Winterize. Perennials that are growing a zone too far north, as well as new or recently transplanted perennials, benefit from the protection of a winter mulch. Wait until the ground is frozen or almost frozen to apply the mulch. Remove it gradually when the ground starts to thaw in the spring.

GROUNDCOVERS:
Choosing Alternatives to a Grass Lawn

If you can't beat it, join it. Rather than battle moss to get grass to grow in a shady area, take pride in a lawn of moss. To encourage moss, remove weeds and leaves diligently. A light application of an acid-balance fertilizer is beneficial to moss, but too much fertilizer will burn the moss and encourage weeds. To increase the size of a moss lawn, remove other plants from the expansion area, save any pieces of moss, and till in plenty of peat moss and compost. Transplant plugs of moss every two or three inches into the new area. Keep the area watered and weeded until the moss takes over.

GROUNDCOVER OPTIONS: **Sweet Woodruff**

Sweet woodruff thrives in moist shade where grass languishes, and adds a touch of the woodland to this backyard suburban tree base.

Nothing compares to grass for sunbathing, tag football, or for providing a fun, safe surface for toddlers and children to frolic upon on a mild summer afternoon. But grass doesn't grow well everywhere, and in some places it's more trouble than it's worth.

Rather than fighting constantly to keep moss and weeds out of a shady area, or living your life in dread of that weekly mowing of a steep, dangerous slope, why not minimize your worries by shrinking your lawn and planting groundcover? Groundcovers are perennials and vines that often require less maintenance than grass, while looking great. They usually don't need to be fertilized or mowed and often require less water than lawns to stay green.

You can get a sense for which groundcovers thrive in your area by observing (and, if possible, getting leaf samples from) nicely landscaped homes in your area. A good garden center should provide more information on groundcovers. But because *groundcovers* is not actually a botanical category, you may not find a groundcover area at your local garden center.

Areas planted to groundcovers described as 'invasive' should have physical barriers between them and other garden areas. Barriers include masonry paths, drives, houses and regularly mowed lawns. Edging material may or may not block groundcovers that spread underground and definitely will not block plants that spread above ground by stolons or rooting branches.

Here's a little exercise to help you decide which areas of your yard should remain planted in grass, and which might be good candidates for groundcover instead.

English Ivy aggressively covers humus-rich slopes, stabilizing the soil and eliminating the need for dangerous lawn maintenance. Keep it weeded and trimmed away from areas where it's not wanted. *NOTE: Ivy and other groundcovers labeled "invasive" may spread uncontrollably if not contained or regularly pruned.*

The Lawn Audit

Walk around your property with a critical eye. Look for places where grass is hard to water or mow, or seems to take extra care to keep healthy and weed free. Narrow strips and islands of grass, dry shady areas, slopes, and areas immediately around the trunks of trees are places that may be candidates for groundcovers or mulch. An area of heavy foot traffic may need a walkway of stone or another durable material.

Trace out the lawn you want to save by cutting its outline with your lawn mower. When possible, avoid sharp angles and isolated peninsulas of lawn, opting for graceful curving lines that are easy to follow with the mower and simple to divide into convenient watering zones.

Make a new lawn plan based on your lawn audit and your needs and desires. Consider mowing time and watering schedules. Ask yourself if the new grass area(s) accommodate the needs of your family. If you are satisfied, it's time to decide how to cover the area that will no longer be lawn.

Pachysandra is easy on the eye in the shady spaces below trees and requires a fraction of the maintenance of grass once it's established.

Blue fescue or sheep fescue, *Festuca ovina glauca*, grows from Zone 5 to 8. Plant blue fescue in full to part sun. This 4 to 12-in. high bunch grass has blue-gray, spiky, bunched foliage and is drought tolerant. Plant 6 to 12 in. apart. Divides well.

Bugleweed or ajuga (ah-joo-guh), *Ajuga reptans*, grows from Zones 3 to 9. Most varieties like part shade, but bronze and purple-leafed varieties thrive in sun. Bugleweed, about 8 in. tall, forms a dense, rapidly spreading mat and develops spikes of blue to violet flowers. This invasive groundcover prefers moist, rich soil. Plant 6 to 12 in. apart. Divides easily.

Chamomile, *Chamaemelum nobile*, grows from Zones 3 to 8 in full sun (preferable) to part shade. It grows 6 to 12 in. high with fine, fragrant foliage and yellow flowers. Chamomile tolerates hot dry conditions and can be mowed and even endures light, occasional foot traffic. It does well between steppingstones. Plant 6 to 12 in. apart. Divides well.

Creeping thyme (time), *Thymus praecox arcticus*, is hardy to Zone 3. This fine-leafed spreading plant prefers full sun. Creeping thyme grows just 3 to 6 in. tall, with aromatic foliage, small leaves, and pink, red, purple or white flowers. It prefers dry, infertile soils and may be stepped on and mowed like a lawn. Creeping thyme is often used between pavers or in the stones of a retaining wall. Plant 6 to 10 in. apart. Divide to propagate.

Leadwort, *Ceratostigma plumbaginoides,* grows in Zones 5 to 9 in full sun to part shade. The 8 to 12-in. plants with shiny green foliage fill in after the soil warms in late spring. Foliage turns reddish in the fall. Half-inch blue flowers bloom from late summer through fall. Tolerates poor, dry soil. Plant 8 to 12 in. apart. Propagate by division in the spring.

Junipers, *Juniperus chinensis, J. horizontalis,* grow in Zones 3 to 9 in full sun. They are low (6 in. to 2 ft., depending on species and variety), spreading, coniferous shrubs with blue-green to gray-green evergreen needles and blue berries. Junipers prefer well-drained, dry soil once established and are very useful for slopes. They are low maintenance. Plant 2 to 5 ft. apart, depending on variety.

Kinnikinnick, manzanita or bearberry, *Arctostaphylus uva-ursi,* grows in full sun in Zones 2 to 10. This is a shrubby plant that grows just 6 to 12 in. high. Kinnikinnick has shiny evergreen foliage, white flowers in spring, and red fruit later. It prefers acid soil and is suited to slopes and windy, dry locations. Deer won't eat it. Plant 1 to 2 ft. apart in late fall or early spring.

Stonecrop sedums, *Sedum spurium, S. kamtschaticum, S. ternatum* and others, grow in Zones 3 to 10 in sun to shade, depending on species and variety. The sedums range from 2 to 24 in. high, but the short, mat-forming varieties like goldmoss stonecrop are most suitable for groundcover. Most spread along the ground with rooting runners. Fleshy evergreen or deciduous (depending on zone) foliage may have red tips and the plants bear yellow or pink flowers. They will grow on poor, rocky and dry soil, tolerating drought. They spread very rapidly under the right conditions and may be invasive. Plant 9 to 12 in. apart. Propagates easily by division.

Creeping lilyturf, *Liriope spicata*, grows from Zone 4 to 10 in sun or shade. The plant spreads underground, forming mounds of grassy leaves 6 to 12 in. high and spikes of lavender to white flowers in summer. Creeping lilyturf tolerates poor soil but not traffic. It is grown mostly in the South. Cut off and compost old growth in spring. Plant 12 in. apart. Divide to propagate.

English Ivy, *Hedera helix*, includes varieties hardy to Zone 5, but more are available in Zones 7 to 9. Plant in deep shade or sun. This spreading, mat-forming vine will cover the ground and any other horizontal or vertical surface. The lobed leaves of English ivy are dark green, yellow, variegated, purple or light green, depending on the variety. Ivy has insignificant flowers. Slow to establish, ivy grows rapidly after the first year. Ivy is very invasive, and can damage the siding of buildings. Plant 12 to 18 in. apart for rapid infill.

Native meadows

An attractive alternative to traditional lawns and planting beds is the meadow of native species. Like native prairies, such plantings comprise a mix of grasses, broadleaf perennials and legumes, a beneficial family of plants that fix nitrogen from the air, thus fertilizing the plant community. The native grasses, like buffalograss and wheatgrass, can be mowed like any other lawn grass and endure foot traffic.

There is a wide variety of plants native to any given area in the United States, so gardeners who wish to create alternative, ecologically-sensitive landscapes have a fine range of cultural options from which to choose.

Native meadow and prairie plants require little water and no fertilizer once they are established. Fertilizing a native planting with nitrogen tends to drive out the legumes and invites weedy species to invade. At first natives need to be kept weeded, but eventually they will hold their own against weeds.

The prairie planting above is suited to full sun locations

in the midwest and plains states. It includes switchgrass, Indiangrass, little bluestem, purple prairie clover, Illinois bundle flower, partridge pea and Maximilian sunflower.

Ferns include various species and genera in a division of plants that once predominated on Earth, and that predates plants that make flowers and seeds. Ferns make neither. Ferns come in sizes from small to gigantic and spread by rhizomes. Each zone has adapted fern species. Most grow well in the deep to part shade of trees. Most prefer humus-rich, acid soils. Ferns mix well with bulbs and many groundcovers. Visit a nursery for adapted species in your area.

Goutweed or bishop's weed, *Aegopodium podagraria,* is hardy to Zone 3 and grows in sun to shade. Goutweed foliage is light green or green and white (variegated) and 12 in. high. Flower stalks shoot up above the foliage in early summer bearing umbels of tiny flowers. The plant spreads aggressively in practically any soil by underground rhizomes. Goutweed responds well to two or three mowings in a year, especially in sun, where old leaves may become brown. The plant is very invasive. Plant 6 to 12 in. apart. Propagate by division.

Hostas or plantain lilies, *Hosta crispula, H. plantaginea* and others, grow in Zones 3 to 9 in part shade and shade, with darker varieties preferring more shade. The plants grow 8 to 24 in. high, depending on variety. Hundreds of varieties are planted mainly for their foliage. Leaves are large to very large and from deep blue-green to yellow-green to variegated. Lavender or white flowers are borne singly on tall stalks, and are relatively small. Some varieties have fragrant flowers and/or flowers that are a little larger and more interesting. Hostas are tolerant of dry soil, but they will look better in rich, moist, well-drained soil. They are easy to divide. Spacing varies.

Lily-of-the-valley, *Convallaria majalis*, grows in Zones 2 to 7 in part shade and shade. Lily-of-the-valley grows 12 in. tall and spreads aggressively by underground rhizomes. Broad, pointed, dark-green leaves accompany arching stems lined with white, fragrant, bell-shaped flowers in late spring. This woodland lily is easily propagated by division. It requires little maintenance but is at its best in rich, moist, well-drained soil. Plant 4 in. apart.

Mondo grasses, *Ophiopogon japonicus* and *O. planiscalpus*, are found mainly in Zones 8 to 10, though some *O. planiscalpus* varieties are hardy to Zone 6. This popular southern groundcover thrives in part sun and shade, but needs protection from midday sun in hot areas. Mondo grass grows 6 to 12 in. tall, depending on species and variety. Leaves are dark green to purple and grass-like. Look for small blue flowers and blue berries, which may be hidden by the foliage. Prefers rich, well-drained soil. May be divided in spring and fall. Space 6 to 12 in. apart, depending on variety.

Pachysandra, *Pachysandra terminalis*, grows in Zones 5 to 8 in the shade. The 8 to 12-in.-high plants grow in spreading clumps. Green and variegated foliage varieties are available; the flowers are insignificant. Likes rich, moist, acid soil. Plant 6 to 8 in. apart in soil amended with peat moss and compost. Apply a mulch. Grows well with other acid-loving woodland plants like azaleas and rhododendrons. Plant 6 in. apart.

Creeping Phlox, *Phlox stolonifera,* grows in Zones 2 through 8 in part to full shade. The 3 to 5-in. plants mix well with other low groundcovers (it is pictured here with *Vinca*). Masses of pink, blue or white flowers bloom in late spring. Prefers moist, fertile soil. Plant 12 to 24 in apart. Propagate by division after flowering.

Green-and-gold or Golden star, *Chrysogonum virginianum*, grows in Zones 5 through 8 in part to full shade (full shade in southern climates). The 8 to 12-in. plants spread by rooting stems and rhizomes. They are evergreen in the South. In the spring, 2-in.-wide yellow flowers bloom heavily, then sporadically all summer. Plant 12 to 18 in. apart in rich, moist soil. Propagate by division in the fall.

Periwinkle or myrtle, *Vinca minor* and *V. major*, is a different species in the North than in the South, though both will grow in Zones 7 and 8. *V. minor* grows from Zones 4 to 8, *V. major* from 7 to 9. *V. minor* is 6 to 12 in. tall, *V. major* can grow up to 2 ft. tall. Both spread above ground in light to moderate shade, tolerating more sun in the North. Both have shiny smallish green or variegated leaves and lilac-blue or white blossoms. The plants cover wet and dry areas, with *V. major* more tolerant of dry soil. Both are invasive. Plant 12 to 18 in. apart.

Spotted lamium or spotted dead nettle, *Lamium maculatum*, grows in Zones 3 through 8 in part sun to deep shade. The plant is 12 to 14 in. high with white or silver and green leaves and pink, lavender, or white flowers. It prefers rich, moist soil, but tolerates dry soil in the shade. Lamium is invasive, spreading aggressively underground by rhizomes. Contain with an edging. Plant 12 to 14 in. apart. May be cut down to 2 to 6 in. once or twice a season to stimulate fresh growth.

Sweet woodruff, *Galium odoratum,* grows from Zones 4 to 8 in part to full shade. Grows 6 to 8 in. tall. Leaves are light green, divided and whorled around the stem. Small, fragrant white flowers grow in open clusters in the spring. Sweet woodruff does best in rich, moist soil. It is aggressive against weeds but compatible with shrubs. Plant 6 in. apart. For a dense, low carpet, trim back mature plants in spring, leaving some growth near the soil.

Wintercreeper, *Euonymus fortunei,* grows north to Zone 4 or 5. The plant likes full sun to deep shade, depending on variety. This low-spreading shrub covers the ground with waxy green foliage that turns dark purple in winter, offsetting the pink fruit. Wintercreeper is a slow-growing, non-invasive groundcover that will cover slopes and require minimal maintenance. Needs no fertilizer and prefers dry soils once established. Plant 1 to 3 ft. apart.

Planting Trees & Shrubs

Trees and shrubs establish the vertical lines of your yard, along with providing many practical benefits (and a few annoyances, depending on how you feel about raking). For best results, plant them right away in the spring so they have a chance to establish before the dormant season.

Balled-and-burlapped plants should be handled by the ball as much as possible to avoid breaking roots near the stem. Only remove twine and pins after positioning the tree or shrub. Remove pots before planting. You may need to cut off a plastic pot with shears or a utility knife. If the roots are densely circled, make three quarter-inch-deep vertical cuts in the pot-ball roots and peel out some of the roots. It is better to plant a little high than a little deep, since deep planting will kill many trees.

Aftercare of Trees & Shrubs

New trees and shrubs should be watered deeply from the start. Leave a soaker hose curled outside the root ball, position a slowly-trickling hose end under the tree for an hour, or fill the basin around the tree one or two times. At first, water once a week or when the soil dries at the surface. Over the season, move to deeper, less frequent watering.

1 Measure from the ground to the point where the stem emerges from the root ball or pot ball. Dig your hole this deep, or a bit shallower. The diameter of the hole should be a third larger than the diameter of the ball. In heavy soils or if you will be mulching, you may plant the root or pot ball a little high, but do not bury the base of the stem.

2 Handle balled-and-burlapped plants by the ball, not the stem, as much as is practical. When the ball is in the hole and positioned correctly, cut off the twine and pull the pins out of the top of the burlap. Fold back the burlap and bend the metal cage off the top of the ball.

3 Fill the space around balled-and-burlapped plants with water before backfilling with dirt. When backfilling, use the water stream from a hose to work dirt into hollow spaces around large root or pot balls. Build a wide berm around the stem of trees and shrubs, using the soil displaced for the hole.

4 Unstable trees should be securely staked with three stakes and tight cords positioned so their directions of force are counter-posed. Run the cord though pieces of old garden hose where they contact the plant and allow room in these loops for the tree to grow.

5 Cover the soil within the berm with three inches of organic mulch, leaving it thinner near the stem. You may want to wrap soaker hose within the berm before laying mulch for more efficient watering.

Pruning Shrubs

Correct pruning improves the health, appearance and performance of woody plants. Pruning can help shrubs develop more and larger flowers. Fruit trees can be induced to grow larger fruit. All woody plants can be aided in attaining a more pleasing shape, and a more appropriate size. By removing misplaced, dead, and oversized branches, storm damage and disease can be reduced, resulting in a healthier, longer-living plant.

Why & When to Thin Shrubs

Thinning, or cutting back, is good for sheared and natural-form shrubs because it allows air and light into the central area of the plant and reduces insect and disease problems. It also removes branches that have been sheared at the same level for years, which can cause them to carry ugly and unhealthy tufts of branchlets. Overgrown deciduous shrubs and some evergreens, whether alone or in hedges, can be completely renovated by clearing out one-third of the wood each year. The best time to thin shrubs is in the early spring, after the wood has thawed but before the buds have broken. You may thin spring-flowering shrubs after they have finished blooming. You may remove dead branches and do very light thinning any time.

How to Thin Shrubs

First, cut dead or damaged branches back to strong living shoots or buds that aim away from the center of the plant. For a major renovation, cut some of the oldest branches on single-trunk shrubs back to the trunk or back to where a branchlet or bud departs from the branch. If the shrub has multiple stems from the ground, you may remove some of the very oldest and almost all of the very youngest right down to the ground. Young stems shooting from roots in the ground are called *suckers,* and should be completely removed, unless you're saving some on a multi-stem plant to replace older stems. Remove any branches that rub and any water sprouts, which are young sprouts that shoot straight up from larger branches. Remove "bottlebrushes" (where numerous branchlets depart from a single stem) at a convenient fork below the bottlebrush. Small gaps left in the foliage will fill in quickly, but try not to create large gaps or remove too much at once—instead plan to prune a little bit each year. Your pile of cuttings should generally not exceed one-third of the shrub's mass, and if you prune lightly on an annual basis, you will need to take much less.

Regular Pruning for Spring-flowering Shrubs

Spring-flowering shrubs may be cut back hard when the flowers begin to fade, to contain the shrub and to increase the size or numbers of flowers that will bloom

1 In general, undertake major pruning in early spring before leaves are out. Your local County Extension Agent or Master Gardener will know when it's safe to prune specific shrubs in your locality. Though in full leaf, this overgrown lilac may be pruned safely in Minnesota.

2 Dead, very small, and overgrown stems may be removed to the ground, leaving a balanced assemblage of healthy, midsized stems.

3 We have removed from 1/3 to 1/2 the biomass of this clump by pruning out conflicting and dead branches as well as whole stems, leaving a graceful stand that affords a view of the yard and reveals the lamppost.

the following year. Forsythia, flowering currant, mock orange, kerria, beauty bush, weigela and spring-flowering spirea are some examples of shrubs that benefit from this post-flowering pruning. Cut off a combination of large and small branches and/or stems to remove about one-third of the total growth. Try to cut branches that are just above another living branch.

NOTE: *Flowering dogwood, potentilla, barberry, magnolias, most viburnum and most lilac prefer to be left alone most years. Hard pruning may result in a year or two with few or no flowers.*

Regular Pruning for Summer- & Winter Flowering Shrubs

Summer- and winter-flowering shrubs produce a lot of growth quickly, then flower from the new growth. You can tell, since the flowers are coming from fresh green or pinkish wood rather than darker, older wood. Examples include peegee hydrangea, crape myrtle, lippia, buddleia, deciduous ceanthus, indigo, summer-flowering spirea and winter-flowering jasmine. Cut all the branches down in early spring to a low framework of branches two or three buds or forks from the ground. This will keep the plants small and the flowers big. Remember not to leave stubs; cut branches in spots where other branches or buds can replace the removed branch.

Prune spring-flowering shrubs, like this spirea, back by one-third when the flowers begin to fade.

Shearing hedges

Shearing with hand shears or electric hedge trimmers cuts back all new growth evenly, producing a dense outer layer. This layer casts shade on the interior of the plant, inhibiting new growth. Consequently, the hedge that is sheared, but not thinned, can only undergo growth in its outer "shell" and is also more vulnerable to disease. To avoid this problem, thin hedges after shearing, taking branches just above points where other buds or branches can replace them.

Shearing is done on an as-needed basis, usually once or twice a year for evergreens and two or three times a year for deciduous shrubs. Do not shear within two months of the first fall frost, since shearing promotes fresh growth that's vulnerable to frost damage.

1 Shear the outer branches to shape the hedge. It's best to shear large-leaf hedges with hand pruners only, since shears will cut many leaves in two, giving the plant a ravaged appearance. Encourage the hedge to grow in a flattened "A" shape, with a slight slope inward from bottom to top. This lets light get to the bottom branches, preventing dieback at the bottom of the hedge.

2 Now, take out dead branches and a few of the bottlebrushes. Leave small gaps in the foliage so light and air can get in to the middle of the plant and promote new growth. Do this only a little bit at each shearing; small gaps will fill in quickly, but large gaps may be difficult to eliminate.

(LEFT) The pole tree trimmer lets you saw and lop high branches while keeping your feet on the ground.

Pruning Trees

Young, growing trees should be pruned a little each year in the late winter or early spring before leaves emerge. Never take too much in a single year, since too much pruning when the tree is dormant will lead to rampant, unhealthy spring growth. Also, the bark of many smooth-barked species is susceptible to sun scald if too much of the canopy is removed. Birches and maples should be pruned in late summer, since they will bleed if pruned in early spring. Generally, prune in the following order:

1) Prune off all dead branches. **2)** Cut off water sprouts and suckers (rapidly growing branches that shoot straight up from much larger branches, the trunk or roots) flush with the branch or root they grow from. It may be necessary to dig down a little to cut a sucker off flush with the root. **3)** If the leader on a small tree or branch forks narrowly, cut off one side of the fork. A narrow fork will make a weak crotch when the two sides become large. Branches that form wide angles with the branch or trunk will be stronger. **4)** Prune branches that grow inward, and remove one of two branches that rub. Prune so the new lead bud or branch is growing away from the center of the tree. **5)** Remove small branches that crowd other branches and branches that are too low on the trunk. Pruning is an ongoing process; so don't try to finish the job in one year. Taking too much at once can kill some trees.

MAKING THE CUT

Use sharp pruners to make a clean cut that slants slightly away from the branch or bud that is not being removed.

A correct cut is made about 1/4-in. above a living branch or bud—close enough to heal over, but not so close that the strength of the crotch is compromised.

Mature trees should be pruned for several reasons: to remove dead, injured or rubbing branches; to keep the tree from catching too much wind and toppling; to eliminate branches that threaten wires, buildings or other property; and to increase sunlight to lawns and gardens. Suckers and water shoots should continue to be removed on adult trees. High and large branches should be pruned professionally for safety reasons.

The Don'ts of Pruning

Don't use tree paint. It interferes with healing. If diseases of your tree species are common in your area, cover the cut with thick paper and masking tape.

Don't "head" a tree. Cutting off the top of a mature tree to keep it small looks like vandalism. Better remove the tree and plant a species of a more appropriate size.

Don't leave stubs. Always try to make cuts where another bud or branch can take over so the wound can heal properly.

THE RIGHT WAY TO CUT OFF A BRANCH

WRONG: Too Long. A branch cut too long will never heal over, which permits rot and disease to enter the tree through the exposed wood.

WRONG: Too Close. Here, the ring is cut away, leaving a gash that could take years to scab over and may introduce disease and rot to the heartwood of the limb.

JUST RIGHT. This cut will allow the injury to heal. Notice the thick ring of living wood that will form the scar tissue.

HOW TO CUT HEAVY BRANCHES

1 Heavy branches need to be cut three times to avoid tearing bark and wood from a tree. Under-cut the branch 6 to 12 in. outside the planned cutting line.

2 Over-cut a little to the outside of the undercut to drop the branch.

3 Cut the remainder of the branch off close to the branch that will remain (See photos, above).

Seasonal Guide to Yard Care

Don't think of spring, summer, fall and winter as being defined purely by their assigned calendar months. These "seasons" are tied to different months in different parts of the country, and can even change from year to year in a single place. Perform lawn and garden chores when the plants are ready for them: not just because the calendar tells you it's March or October. In the following pages, we'll describe each season to help you perform garden chores at the right time. But look over the guide for the subseason immediately prior to and following the one you're in. You might find chores that need to be done right now in your yard.

Seasonal Guide to Yard Care

Late Winter, Early Spring

Late winter or early spring is marked by melting snow (if you get it), softening earth, swelling buds and the return of early songbirds. This season starts in January or February in the South and may not start until April or May in the far North.

Trees and Shrubs: Prune dead branches from any woody plant. Prune living wood of evergreens, trees, vines, summer-flowering shrubs and winter-flowering shrubs after the wood thaws but before new growth. Do not prune bleeding trees, like birches and maples, and don't prune spring-flowering shrubs now. Wait to prune tropicals like hibiscus to avoid stimulating early growth. Feed with compost or a slow-release fertilizer if needed, but wait until late spring to spread a thick mulch. Plant bare-root trees and shrubs as soon as you can.

Perennials: Remove winter mulch. In places where the ground freezes solid under winter mulch, gradually remove the mulch as it thaws. In places where the mulch keeps the ground from freezing, gradually remove the mulch when the plants under it begin to grow. Cut down and remove dead plant material. Evergreen ground-covers may be mowed or cut back and raked to remove dead or old growth. Divide perennials if the ground can be worked. In areas with mild and rainy winters such as the Pacific West, fall may be a better time to divide perennials, though a wet early spring is a good second choice.

Lawns: You may overseed cool-season grass seed in the North. If you will be working the soil, however, wait until mid-spring when the soil is dry enough to till. Pull or spot-treat cool-season weeds in the South. Apply preemergent herbicides only if needed to dormant, warm-season lawns before the spring flush of annual weeds, but not if you will be dethatching or aerating later, since these procedures will eliminate the effects of the herbicide. If you will be planting a warm-season lawn, begin taking soil samples.

Mid-spring

Daffodils are blooming, cool-season grasses are growing, and some early leaves and the flowers of early shrubs are emerging. You may still have a late frost in northern areas.

Shrubs, Vines and Trees: Plant bare-root trees and shrubs in areas where it's still moist and cool, and plant balled-and-burlapped and containered trees, shrubs and hardy vines anywhere, although fall and winter is a better choice in mild areas with a winter rainy season. Begin shearing hedges as needed in the South. Keep newly planted woody plants watered.

Perennials: Remove mulch, cut back old dead growth, and rake debris. Divide perennials where cool, moist conditions will prevail for a month or more. Fertilize and/or spread compost or rotted manure, but wait to mulch until the soil warms up. Plant containered perennials anywhere, although fall is preferable in mild areas with a winter rainy season. Keep new perennials watered. Begin weeding.

Lawn: Sharpen your lawn mower if it was not done in fall; buy new gas; service your lawn mower if it was not done in fall. Raking, pulling and digging young perennial weeds will save a lot of work later. Check for grub infestations, if this has been a problem, and apply biological controls if needed.

Mow warm-season grasses low the first time and rake for the first time to remove old brown growth. Aerate and dethatch warm-season grasses after the third mowing. If you will be planting a new warm-season lawn, eliminate weeds with glyphosate when temperatures allow. If the ground is prepared, you may lay sod, or plant sprigs or plugs for a warm-season lawn, but it's still too early for seeding in most of the South.

Begin mowing cool-season grasses, but mow high to discourage germinating weeds. Aerate cool-season grasses, if needed, and apply compost. Fertilize cool-season grasses if needed, though fall is a better time if you only fertilize once or twice. Continue to work on bare spots and uneven spots on a cool-season lawn. Apply preemergent herbicides only if needed to cool-season grasses now, or a bit later before warm-season weeds like crabgrass germinate (but after performing any mechanical treatment, like aerating or dethatching, which will deactivate the herbicide).

Late Spring

Leaves are almost fully expanded, spring-blooming trees and shrubs are in full flower and may be starting to fade. Evergreens are sprouting new growth. Lawns are growing full tilt.

Shrubs, Vines and Trees: Prune early-flowering shrubs when the flowers fade. Deadhead rhododendrons and azaleas for better blossoms next year. Shear evergreens and deciduous shrubs if needed, leaving some new growth on the plants. Continue to water newly planted shrubs, vines and trees. Spread mulch.

Perennials: Shear faded flowers that bloom in masses and deadhead larger, faded flowers. Continue to plant containered perennials if you can keep them moist. Plant cold-sensitive annuals now also, when you are sure you are past the last frost date. Divide daffodils. Cultivate and pull weeds. Keep new plants watered. Spread mulch.

Lawns: Warm-season grasses are growing now and may be dethatched, aerated, and fertilized or spread with compost. Late spring is a good time to plant or make repairs to warm-season lawns using sod, plugs or sprigs. In warmer parts of the South you can seed warm-season grasses now. Keep new cool-season and new warm-season grasses watered. Established grass should be watered deeply and allowed to dry between waterings. Mow when lawn grass grows one-third higher than its optimal height. Most cool-season grasses may continue to be mowed high to fight weeds. Control caterpillar worms and grubs if levels are unacceptable.

Early Summer

Gardens, lawns and weeds grow vigorously in the warm, often wet weather of early summer. Nights are warm. This is a good time to start a compost pile.

Shrubs, Vines and Trees: Prune early-flowering shrubs when the flowers fade. Remove suckers and water sprouts from the roots and stems of trees and shrubs. Shear evergreens and deciduous shrubs if needed. Continue to water newly-planted shrubs, vines and trees. Pick and destroy pest beetles.

Perennials: Shear faded flowers that bloom in masses and deadhead larger, faded flowers. Cultivate and pull weeds. Keep new plants watered and water established plants deeply if needed. Apply mulch.

Lawns: Warm-season grasses may be dethatched, aerated, top-dressed and fertilized if needed and you have not done this yet. Keep new cool-season and new warm-season grasses watered. Established grass should be watered deeply and allowed to dry between waterings. Continue to mow when lawn grass grows one-third taller than its optimal height. Plant warm-season grasses by any method now, since it's warm enough for the seed (although new seed will require watering multiple times during the day when it doesn't rain). Most cool-season grasses may continue to be mowed high to resist drought or shade-out stress. Spray for caterpillar worms and grubs if needed. Take soil samples if you will be planting a cool-season lawn in late summer.

Mid-summer

Mid-summer is often hot and dry in much of the country, slowing growth and browning grass. Parts of the Deep South have a mid-summer rainy season, where it's a good time for establishing new lawns.

Shrubs, Vines and Trees: Prune early-flowering shrubs that are now finishing flowering. Shear evergreens and deciduous shrubs if needed. Continue to water newly-planted shrubs, vines and trees. Deadhead flowering vines. Prune suckers and water sprouts as needed.

Perennials: Deadhead faded flowers on perennials and annuals. Cultivate and pull weeds. Keep new plants watered, and water established plants deeply if needed. A diseased or ragged groundcover may be sheared to the ground and allowed to re-grow.

Lawns: Keep new warm-season grasses watered; established grass should be watered deeply and allowed to dry between waterings. Continue to mow when lawn grass grows one-third taller than its optimal height. You may provide a slow-release, high-nitrogen or only-nitrogen fertilizer to actively-growing grass in the South. Plant warm-season grasses, especially if you have a mid-summer rainy season that is conducive to starting lawns at this time. Cool-season grasses may continue to be mowed high to resist drought, summer weeds, or to shade-out sun stress. Take soil samples if you will be planting a cool-season lawn in the fall. Kill old grass with an herbicide if you will be planting in late summer. Control caterpillar worms and grubs as necessary.

Late Summer

Days are getting shorter and the sun is less intense, but some hot days are still in store. Now is a good time for lawn and garden work because cooler weather is just around the corner.

Shrubs, Vines and Trees: Early August is the last safe time to shear evergreens and deciduous shrubs in much of the North, since shearing stimulates tender growth that may be damaged by frost. Continue to water newly-planted shrubs, vines and trees. Prune maples, birches and other deciduous trees that tend to bleed if pruned in early spring. Oaks, elms and other disease-susceptible trees should only be pruned in the winter or early spring. New woody plants are easy to plant and establish now.

Perennials: Deadhead faded flowers on perennials and annuals. Keep new plants watered, and water established plants deeply if needed. Begin cutting back spent plants. Divide perennials that are done blooming in short-season northern areas to give them plenty of time to take root before winter (fall-blooming perennials should be divided in the spring). Plant containered perennials.

Lawns: Grass should be watered deeply and allowed to dry between waterings. Continue to mow when lawn grass grows one-third taller than its optimal height. Most cool-season grasses may continue to be mowed high. Plant warm-season grasses in hot parts of the Southwest that experience a rainy season now or in early fall. Preemergent herbicides may be applied in the Middle South and transition zones to control germination of winter weeds in warm-season grass (but only if these are a problem and not if you will be overseeding in the fall). Consult local authorities to learn the best time to apply preemergent herbicides in your area. Begin killing the old grass if you will be planting a new cool-season lawn. Where winters come early, this is the best time for planting a new cool-season lawn or repairing an old one, and also for aerating, dethatching, overseeding, and topdressing a cool-season lawn.

Early Fall

Early fall is gentle with plants, making it a popular time for working with perennials and cool-season lawns.

Trees, Vines and Shrubs: In temperate climates, prune maples, birches and other deciduous trees that tend to bleed if pruned in the spring. Early fall is a good time to plant woody plants in most of the country, though you might hold off until the winter rains in California.

Perennials: This is a good time to plant spring-flowering bulbs and containered plants of all kinds almost everywhere. Divide early-blooming perennials in the South as you get a break from the heat, but still have two or three months for the plants to establish before winter. In the Southwest, a break from summer heat and a little more rain make this a good time to plant and divide a wide range of perennials. You may wait for the rainy season to divide plants in the Pacific West. Keep any transplants watered. Fall-blooming perennials will be showing their colors and may be planted for immediate gratification North and South.

Lawns: Wherever cool-season grasses are the primary lawn type, this is the best time to: plant a new cool-season lawn or make repairs to an old one; fertilize cool-season lawns; and aerate, dethatch, overseed and top-dress a cool-season lawn.

Apply preemergent herbicides for winter weeds on warm-season lawns in the South if this is needed and if you will not be overseeding with a winter grass. You may overseed for a green winter lawn in early fall in the Mid-south, the transition zones, and some other parts of the South. Begin mowing a warm-season grass to the maximum height for the species. You may apply a complete fall fertilizer high in nitrogen and potassium in the Deep South.

Middle Fall

The cleanup season is upon us in most of the country. Fall color is in full swing and leaves are falling.

Trees, Shrubs and Vines: Plant containered woody plants in most areas.

Perennials: When herbaceous plants die back, chop them back a few inches from the ground and rake out the debris. Fall-blooming perennials may be kept going. You may still plant bulbs and containered plants, which go on sale in the North. Water new transplants if they are still growing. Outdoor clay flowerpots should be emptied of soil and stored.

Lawns: You may overseed for a green winter lawn in the South; this may happen as late as November in Southern California and other very mild areas. Reduce mowing height for the last mowing in the North if fungal disease is a problem. Increase mowing height in the South to the maximum for your warm-season species or for the recommended height for an overseeded cool-season grass.

In the North, drain irrigation systems and water features. Shut down and drain outside water spigots and pipes. Winterize your lawn mower. Clean out any sprayers and note which chemical they were used to apply. Drain and hang hoses for the winter. Rake and compost leaves.

Late Fall

Leaves have fallen. Perhaps an early snow has blanketed a northern state. In the Temperate South, most plants have entered winter dormancy. In Southern California and the Gulf States winter plants are coming into their own.

Trees, Vines and Shrubs: In the North, evergreen shrubs may be protected from winter drying with burlap or antidesiccant sprays. Protect the trunks of young trees against rodents and sunscald with plastic tree wraps. Any delicate woody plant may be protected from heavy loads of snow with a protective structure. In the Pacific Northwest, you may prune summer-flowering trees and shrubs in late fall. In Southern California and other areas with mild, wet winters, plant bare-root trees, shrubs and vines now, as well as any containered woody plants.

Perennials: Finish cutting and removing dead growth from beds, but you may wish to leave any that look good in the winter. Apply mulch to tender or new plants after a few hard freezes. If you apply mulch too early, rodents may build nests in it. In areas with mild, wet winters, such as in the Pacific West, you may divide perennials in November and December.

Lawns: Rake any leaves off the grass. Finish winterizing chores. Sharpen and oil all tools. Fertilize with NPK (nitrogen, phosphorous, potassium) in the North if you normally fertilize twice and have already fertilized in late summer: it gives the grass a good start in the spring without assisting spring weeds. In the South, mow overseeded cool-season grasses to the correct height for the species.

Winter

Much of California and parts of the Southwest experience a rainy season in the winter, and enjoy lush growth of winter plants. If you live elsewhere, try not to think about this.

Shrubs, Vines and Trees: Shovel heavy snow from hedges. Prune woody plants in the South, including Southern California, but wait until the wood thaws in early spring in the North. Do not prune spring-flowering plants anywhere now, since this would remove the flower buds. In Southern California, plant shrubs, vines and trees in December or early January so these may establish in the rainy season.

Lawns: Mow overseeded southern lawns to the height recommended for the cool-season grass used. Pull or spot-apply herbicides for winter weeds.

Index

A

A. canadense (See Garlic)
A. stolonifera (See Creeping Bentgrass)
Accent plantings, designing, 124-125
Aegopodium podagraria (See Goutweed)
Aerating, 116-117
Aerator, manual, 117
  power core, 21, 62, 116
Agropyron repens (See Quackgrass)
Agrostis tenuis (See Colonial Bentgrass)
Air filters, for lawn mowers, 26, 30
Ajuga reptans (See Bugleweed)
Allium vineale (See Garlic)
Annual Bluegrass, 103
Annual Ryegrass, 43
Aphids (See Greenbugs)
Arctostaphylus uva-ursi (See Kinnikinnick)
Armyworm (See Insects, Armyworm)

B

Bacillus popillae, 107
Bacillus thuringiensis, 107
Bahiagrass, 41
Bamboo, 100
Bare spots, planting, 121
Bearberry (See Kinnikinnick)
Beauveria bassiana, 107
Bermudagrass, 36, 41, 50, 61, 105
Billbugs (See Insects, Billbugs)
Bindweed, 50
Bishop's weed (See Goutweed)
Black Medic, 103
Blower, 19
Blue Fescue, 140
Blue Gramagrass, 39, 41
Branches, cutting, 151
Brick edging, 130-131
Brown Patch, 114
Bt (See *Bacillus thuringiensis*)
Buchloe dactyloides (See Buffalograss)
Buffalograss, 39, 41
Bugleweed, 140

C

Caliche, 54
Canada Thistle, 101
Caterpillar worms (See Insects, caterpillar worms)
Cenchrus pauciflorus (See Sandbur)
Centipedegrass, 41, 61
Ceratostigma plumbaginoides (See Leadwort)
Chamaemelum nobile (See Chamomile)

Chamomile, 140
Chewings Fescue, 45, 47
Chinch bugs (See Insects, Chinch bugs)
Chrysogonum virginianum (See Green-and-gold)
Cirsium arvense (See Canada Thistle)
Clover (See White Clover)
Coastal Deep South lawn zone, 34-35
Colonial Bentgrass, 46-47
Common Chickweed, 103
Compost, 56, 62, 65, 66
Convallaria majalis (See Lily-of-the-valley)
Crabgrass, 50, 104
Creeping Bentgrass, 46-47
Creeping Charlie (See Ground Ivy)
Creeping Lilyturf, 142
Creeping Phlox, 144
Creeping Thyme, 140
Cutworm (See Insects, Cutworm)
Cynodon dactylon (See Bermudagrass)
Cynodon dactylon x C. transvalensis (See Bermudagrass)
Cyperus esculentus (See Nutsedge)

D

D. sanguinalis (See Crabgrass)
Dandelion digger, 98
Dandelions, 100, 102
Deadheading, 137
Dethatcher, 109
Dethatching, 118-119
Diatomaceous Earth, 108
Dicots, 100
Digitaria ischaemum (See Crabgrass)
Dollar Spot, 114
Drainage, 54-55
Drainage pipe, 54
Drainage tile, 54, 55
Drip lines (See Sprinkler, in-ground, drip lines)
Dry wells, 54, 55

E

E. supine (See Spurges)
Ecolawn, 47
Edger, manual, 15, 95
  power, 21, 95
Edging, 95
Electric power yard tools, 19
English Ivy, 139, 142
Epimedium, 126
Eremochloa ophiuroides (See Centipedegrass)
Ergonomic tools, 10
Euonymus fortunei (See Wintercreeper)
Euphorbia maculata (See Spurges)

F

F. longifolia (See Hard Fescue)
F. ovina (See Sheep Fescue)
F. rubra commutata (See Chewings Fescue)
Fall yard care tips, 156-157
Ferns, 143
Fertilizer, 56, 62, 70-75
  application advice, 73
  buying, 72
  calculation table, 71
  estimating needs, 72
  label analysis, 72
  spreading, 74
  timing, 75
Festuca arundinaciea (See Tall Fescue)
Festuca ovina glauca (See Blue Fescue)
Festuca rubra (See Red Fescue)
Fire ants (See Insects, Fire ants)
Forged steel handle attachments, 11
Fork, 14
  garden, 14, 128
  manure, 14
  mulch, 14
  spading, 14
Freedom lawn, 77
French drains (See Dry wells)
Fungicide, 114-115

G

Garlic, 101
Glechoma hederacea (See Ground Ivy)
Glyphosate, 50, 57, 128
Golden Star (See Green-and-gold)
Gophers, 113
Goutweed, 143
Grading, 52-53, 121
Grass, 32-47
  bunch, 32
  cool-season, 32, 42-47
    fertilizer timing, 75
  creeping, 32
  cross section of, 33
  types, 32-47
  warm-season, 32, 36-41
    fertilizer timing, 75
  zones, 34-35
Grass diseases, 114-115
Grass seed, 58-63
Grass shears (See Shears, grass)
Green Foxtail, 102
Green-and-gold, 144
Greenbugs, 113
Ground Ivy, 98, 102
Groundcover, 127, 138-145
  types, 139-145
Gypsum, 56

H

Hand cultivator, 14

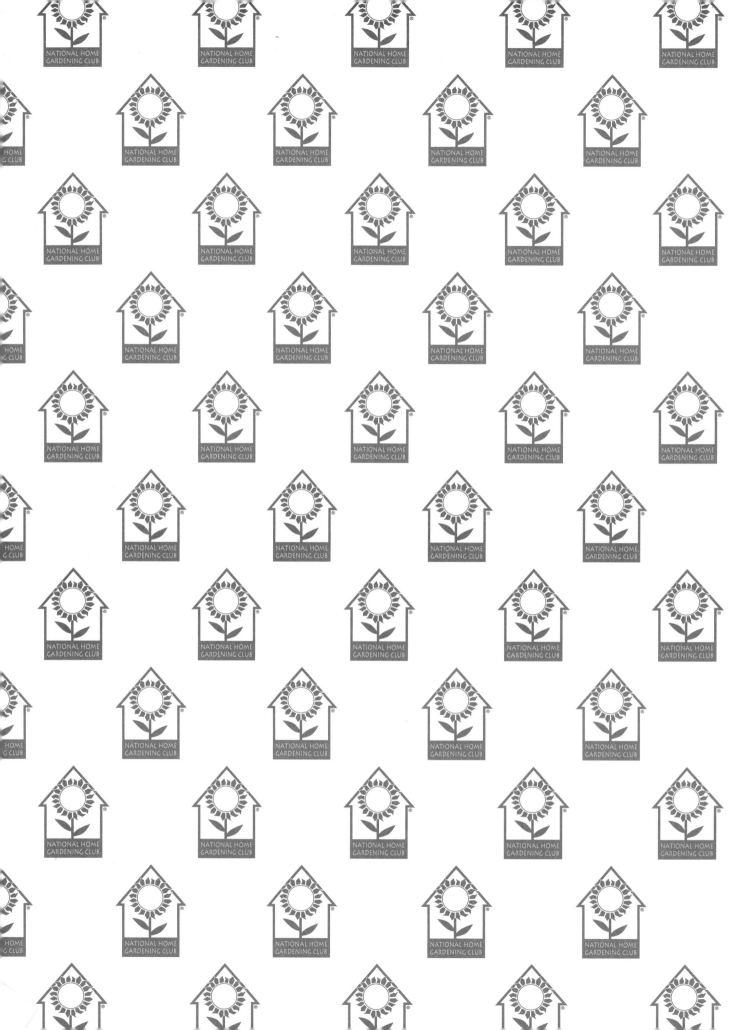